NEW DIRECTIONS FOR STUDENT SERVICES

Margaret J. Barr, *Northwestern University*
EDITOR-IN-CHIEF

M. Lee Upcraft, *The Pennsylvania State University*
ASSOCIATE EDITOR

Men and Rape: Theory, Research, and Prevention Programs in Higher Education

Alan D. Berkowitz
Hobart and William Smith Colleges

EDITOR

Number 65, Spring 1994

JOSSEY-BASS PUBLISHERS
San Francisco

This volume is dedicated to the many women who have been victims of unwanted sexual experiences and to those men who are working to prevent women's future victimization.

MEN AND RAPE: THEORY, RESEARCH, AND PREVENTION PROGRAMS
IN HIGHER EDUCATION
Alan D. Berkowitz (ed.)
New Directions for Student Services, no. 65
Margaret J. Barr, Editor-in-Chief
M. Lee Upcraft, Associate Editor

Microfilm copies of issues and articles are available in 16mm and 35mm, as well as microfiche in 105mm, through University Microfilms Inc., 300 North Zeeb Road, Ann Arbor, Michigan 48106-1346.

LC 85-644751   ISSN 0164-7970   ISBN 0-7879-9971-7

NEW DIRECTIONS FOR STUDENT SERVICES is part of The Jossey-Bass Higher and Adult Education Series and is published quarterly by Jossey-Bass Inc., Publishers, 350 Sansome Street, San Francisco, California 94104-1342 (publication number USPS 449-070). Second-class postage paid at San Francisco, California, and at additional mailing offices. POSTMASTER: Send address changes to New Directions for Student Services, Jossey-Bass Inc., Publishers, 350 Sansome Street, San Francisco, California 94104-1342.

SUBSCRIPTIONS for 1994 cost $47.00 for individuals and $62.00 for institutions, agencies, and libraries.

EDITORIAL CORRESPONDENCE should be sent to the Editor-in-Chief, Margaret J. Barr, 633 Clark Street, 2-219, Evanston, Illinois 60208-1103.

Cover photograph by Wernher Krutein/PHOTOVAULT © 1990.

Manufactured in the United States of America. Nearly all Jossey-Bass books, jackets, and periodicals are printed on recycled paper that contains at least 50 percent recycled waste, including 10 percent postconsumer waste. Many of our materials are also printed with vegetable-based inks; during the printing process, these inks emit fewer volatile organic compounds (VOCs) than petroleum-based inks. VOCs contribute to the formation of smog.

CONTENTS

EDITOR'S NOTES

Men have a responsibility to prevent rape. This volume provides resources for professionals in higher education who want to work with college men to reduce the incidence of sexual assault and rape, especially acquaintance rape, on U.S. campuses. The chapters in this volume offer a philosophy for effective rape prevention work, review relevant research and theory, evaluate resource materials, provide guidelines for clinical interventions, and introduce a model acquaintance rape prevention program for men.

U.S. colleges and universities devote considerable attention and resources to issues of sexual coercion and assault. On most campuses, the effects of rape are combated through the development of policies that define objectionable behavior and appropriate sanctions and the provision of clinical and advocacy services for victims. Colleges' and universities' attempts at rape prevention have resulted in a variety of coeducational workshops and programs, yet the handful of program evaluation studies that have been conducted raise questions about the effectiveness, for both men and women, of programs provided to mixed-gender audiences. In addition, because most rape prevention programs emphasize facts and provision of information, they are often conducted in an intellectual vacuum without adequate attention to the theoretical, research, and clinical treatment literatures on rape proclivity among men. These literatures converge in two important conclusions: first, it is the experience of masculinity itself—how men think of themselves as men—that creates the psychological and cultural environment that leads men to rape, and second, this environment is perpetuated through men's relationships with and expectations of each other. Programs that address all-male groups and incorporate these two insights into program activities and interventions are clearly exceptions to current practice.

This volume begins with a comprehensive review by me, Barry Burkhart, and Susan Bourg of the empirical research literature on college men's proclivity for rape and sexual assault. The studies we review in Chapter One suggest that almost all men are at risk of committing rape, owing to their socialization and life experience. Chapter Two, by Rocco Capraro, examines current perspectives on the culture of masculinity in order to develop a rape prevention philosophy based on men's experience. This focus on men's experience runs through all the chapters. Chapters Three, Four, and Five translate theory and research into particular educational and clinical strategies. In Chapter Three, I offer guidelines for a model rape prevention/education program based on an effective workshop conducted at Hobart College. In Chapter Four, Adam Simon, Jack Paris, and Charles Ramsay offer three student perspectives on facilitating such a program. Clinical treatment guidelines for perpetrators are reviewed in Chapter Five by Jeffrey Pollard. The interventions described acknowledge the powerful influence men have on each other and find ways for men to use this influence to promote men's positive change and action against rape. Chapter Six, by Barry Burkhart, Susan Bourg, and me, discusses methodological problems in rape prevention research and recommends a new research agenda that will examine prosocial, anti-rape behaviors among men. In Chapter Seven, James Earle and Charles Nies review and evaluate selected video programs and written materials that can be incorporated into all-male educational programs for college men and into facilitator training programs. Finally, the Appendix to this volume contains an outline of the model rape prevention program described in Chapter Three.

Throughout this volume, the authors employ feminine pronouns in referring to victims/survivors and masculine pronouns in referring to perpetrators. Although rape can create male victims/survivors, occur between individuals of the same gender, and be perpetrated by women, our usage is justified by the fact that the overwhelming majority of campus rapes are perpetrated by men against women.

I am extremely grateful to have worked with the eight men and one woman who have contributed to this volume. The fact that these men and many others around the country have committed themselves to the eradication of sexual violence suggests cautious optimism for the future, and we hope that this work will inspire similar efforts among others. We are also grateful for the tremendous intellectual and moral inspiration we have received from feminist scholarship and from the women survivors and advocates who have worked so hard to give sexual assault and rape the attention they deserve.

Finally, I must note the potential limitations of this volume. Virtually all of the empirical research, clinical treatment approaches, and intervention strategies available have focused on men without specifying these men's differences in sexual orientation and ethnicity. As a result, specific information is lacking on the incidence and prevention of acquaintance rape among gay and ethnic minority populations. A new generation of research, clinical work, and program development is required to determine whether approaches developed for a generic audience of men can be adapted to more narrowly defined populations as well.

Alan D. Berkowitz
Editor

ALAN D. BERKOWITZ is counseling center director and assistant professor of psychology at Hobart and William Smith Colleges.

A discussion of recent studies on college men as sexual assault and rape perpetrators accompanies recommendations and an integrative theoretical model to be used in rape prevention programs designed for college men.

Research on College Men and Rape

Alan D. Berkowitz, Barry R. Burkhart, Susan E. Bourg

Considerable research has been devoted to identifying the attitudes, behaviors, and characteristics of college men who rape. Substantial numbers of college women are at risk of becoming victims of acquaintance rape, with prevalence figures ranging from 15 to 44 percent (Lundberg-Love and Geffner, 1989). Even greater numbers of undergraduate women experience other forms of sexual assault, with one study reporting rates of sexually coercive experiences as high as 96 percent (Skelton, 1982). There is a consensus among researchers that few of these sexual assaults and rapes are reported to campus authorities or identified as assaults or rapes by the victim or perpetrator. This finding has led some researchers to describe acquaintance rape as "the hidden crime" (Koss, 1988; Parrot and Bechhofer, 1991). Similarly, college men who engage in sexual coercion have been described as "hidden" or "undetected" offenders (Koss, Leonard, Beezley, and Oros, 1985, p. 983). Although heterosexual men are perpetrators and women the victims in almost all cases, there is evidence that acquaintance rape on campus may occur at similar rates among gay men and lesbian women (Baier, Rosenzweig, and Whipple, 1991).

This chapter reviews literature on heterosexual college men as perpetrators of sexual assault, including acquaintance rape, with particular emphasis on research completed since 1980. We first describe a model for an integrated theory of sexual assault and acquaintance rape. This model also supplies a context for our ensuing discussion of research on four aspects of male

---

This chapter is an expansion and revision of "College Men as Perpetrators of Acquaintance Rape and Sexual Assault: A Review of Recent Research," by Alan D. Berkowitz, which appeared in the *Journal of American College Health*, 1992, *40*, 175–181.

NEW DIRECTIONS FOR STUDENT SERVICES, no. 65, Spring 1994 © Jossey-Bass Publishers

perpetration of sexual assault: the definition and incidence of sexual assault and rape, perpetrator characteristics, situational variables, and men's misperceptions of women's sexual intent. We conclude by discussing the implications of the research literature for the development of effective rape prevention programs for men.

Sexual assault occurs when one person is sexually intimate with another without that other person's full consent. Sexually assaultive behaviors can be placed on a continuum according to the degree of force or coercion involved. Thus, they range from a perpetrator's ignoring indications that intimacy is unwanted to his threatening negative consequences or use of force to his actually using force to obtain sexual intimacy. Rape is the most extreme form of sexual assault and is legally defined in most states as penetration without consent.

Integrated Model of Sexual Assault and Acquaintance Rape

Various theoretical models have been proposed to explain the occurrence of sexual assault. Some researchers and theorists have suggested that sexual assault results from normal socialization processes for men in this culture. This sociocultural approach places rape on a continuum of sexually assaultive behaviors, without defining it as a deviant act committed by atypical individuals (Margolin, Miller, and Moran 1989). A considerable amount of research supports this model (Koss, Gidycz, and Wisniewski, 1987; Koss, Leonard, Beezley, and Oros, 1985; Malamuth, 1986; Rapaport and Burkhart, 1984).

Other theoretical models have focused on the personality characteristics and behaviors of the perpetrator or the victim, situations in which assaults are more likely to occur, and patterns of misinterpretation and miscommunication about sexual intimacy between women and men. As evidence documenting the importance of all of these variables has accrued, researchers have formulated and tested multivariate models of sexual assault that take into consideration the relative roles of these different variables. Multivariate models can be used to explain differences among men in variables related to the likelihood of committing a sexual assault and to identify men with a greater propensity to rape.

Our proposed model of sexual assault (Figure 1.1) considers the relative influences of perpetrator characteristics, situational variables associated with sexual assault, perpetrator misperceptions of a victim's sexual intent, and characteristics associated with women who have an increased risk of victimization. Although a discussion of women's risk factors for victimization is outside the scope of this review, a considerable literature exists on this topic (Harney and Muehlenhard, 1991; Mandoki and Burkhart, 1991; Koss and Dinero, 1989a). As Figure 1.1 illustrates, the model posits a possible causal relationship

Figure 1.1. Integrative Model of Sexual Assault and Acquaintance Rape

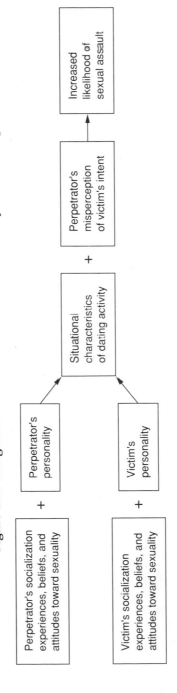

Source: Berkowitz, 1992, p. 176.

between the different variables. A perpetrator's attitudes, beliefs, and social-ization experiences define the conditions in which he would be willing to sex-ually assault an acquaintance or would believe that sexual assault was justifiable. These attitudes and beliefs may serve as heuristics in a perpetrator's decision making (Burkhart and Fromuth, 1991) allowing rapid, biased pro-cessing of attributions and decisions in sexual contexts. Other perpetrator char-acteristics, including personality and previous sexual experiences, enhance a man's willingness to act on his beliefs and attitudes. Finally, situational vari-ables—actual occurrences in the context of a date or social interaction—serve as triggers for the perpetrator, leading him to ignore or misinterpret his part-ner's sexual intent. This model assumes that most men who commit rape and other forms of sexual assault do not define their behavior as assault and are, therefore, able to justify their actions to themselves and others, rendering themselves hidden offenders. The unwillingness or inability of rapists to define their behavior as coercive has been documented in a number of studies (Koss, 1988; Box, 1983; Koss and Leonard, 1984).

Incidence of Male Sexual Assault

Considerable research has examined the frequency of sexual assaults commit-ted by college men, with studies indicating that 25 to 60 percent of these men have engaged in some form of sexually coercive behavior. In one study by Rapaport and Burkhart (1984), only 39 percent of males sampled denied coer-cive involvement, 28 percent admitted having used a coercive method at least once, and 15 percent admitted to forcing a woman to have intercourse at least once. Koss and others, using data from a large, nationally representative sam-ple of college and university students, found that 25 percent of male respon-dents had committed some form of sexual assault since age fourteen (Koss, Gidycz, and Wisniewski, 1987; Koss, 1988; Koss and Dinero, 1989b).

The perpetration of sexual assault by college men has also been examined in relation to a variety of predisposing factors. In one study, 57 percent of the men surveyed admitted to perpetrating sexual assault, with 51 percent report-ing an incident during college (Muehlenhard and Linton, 1987). In this study and another by Rapaport and Burkhart (1984), the most frequent means men employed was to ignore the victim's protests and no's. Koss (1988) and Koss, Gidycz, and Wisniewski (1987) noted that college men's admissions of sexual assault did not account for all the sexual victimization experiences reported to the researchers and that the difference was due to underreporting by perpe-trators rather than to the victimizing of large numbers of women by only a few extremely sexually active men.

Men also report engaging in unwanted sex. Muehlenhard and Cook (1988) found that almost two-thirds of the college men they surveyed had engaged in unwanted intercourse, primarily due to male peer pressure or wanting to be popular. Similar results were obtained in another study in which 14 percent of male students reported having been forced to have intercourse against their will, and 17 percent indicated that they had been pressed to have other forms of sexual contact when they did not want to (Aizenman and Kelley, 1988).

Perpetrator Characteristics

Men grow up in an environment that supports the objectification of women and encourages occasionally violent and coercive behavior. Many college men admit a willingness to commit sexual assault under certain conditions, and to a degree, these assaults logically follow from men's socialization into traditional gender roles. However, men's gender socialization experiences cannot be the sole explanation of sexual assault because many men do not act on these cultural messages. Rape-supportive attitudes and beliefs may create a potential for engaging in sexual assault acted upon only by men with particular personality characteristics and sexual histories. Studies that evaluate the role of different factors in predisposing men to condone or engage in sexually aggressive acts are summarized in the following sections.

Male Socialization. Many theorists have argued that the socialization of U.S. men encourages a complex of attitudes and behaviors that predispose men to dominate and abuse women. Brannon's analysis (1976) of the male sex role found that it required men to avoid acting in ways that could be seen as feminine ("no sissy stuff"); to strive for power, status, and control ("be a big wheel"); to act tough and unemotional ("be a sturdy oak"); and to be aggressive and take risks ("give 'em hell") (p. 12). Men's sexuality and their relationships with women provide a sphere for the enactment and confirmation of these traditional gender-role expectations, which assign men the role of aggressor and women the role of gatekeeper in sexual intimacy. O'Neil (1990) has referred to the totality of these male sex-role behaviors and attitudes as the "masculine mystique" (p. 26). Sex-role socialization thus gives men permission to commit sexual abuse, creating a cognitive framework for assault's justification. Gender socialization is the foundation for sexual aggression (Burkhart and Fromuth, 1991), acting to normalize and promote rape by encouraging men to adopt rape-supportive beliefs and patterns of action conducive to sexual aggression (Burkhart and Stanton, 1988).

Williams and Holmes (1981) argue that rape is the result of differential and unequal masculine and feminine sex-role socialization from birth, with men's being socialized to emphasize force, dominance, and sexual conquest as a means of demonstrating their masculinity to themselves and others. Men feel pressure from other men to be sexual in order to confirm their masculinity. Thus, sexually aggressive behavior may result from the intense social pressure for males to be masculine (Erway, 1990; Groth, 1979; West, Roy, and Nichols,

1978; Kanin, 1965, 1967, 1983, 1984, 1985) as well as from perceived pressure from peers (Aizenman and Kelley, 1988; Muehlenhard and Cook, 1988). These dual pressures lead men to emphasize their sexual experiences in conversation with other men, even though many may be uncomfortable with such discourse (Berkowitz, in press), and contribute to men's participation in sexual encounters that may later be regretted.

Attitudes and Rape Myths. Socialization into masculinity provides men with attitudes and systems of belief that allow them to justify or deny their sexual assaults. Thus, in some research, men who accepted stereotypical myths about rape, viewed relationships between men and women as adversarial, condoned violence against women, or held traditional attitudes about sex roles were found to be more tolerant of rape, more blaming of rape victims, and more likely to rape if they could ensure that no one would find out as compared with men who did not hold these views (Koss, Leonard, Beezley, and Oros, 1985; Muehlenhard and Linton, 1987; Reilly, Lott, Caldwell, and DeLuca, 1991). Adherence to rape-supportive attitudes is also associated with previous perpetration (Koss, Leonard, Beezley, and Oros, 1985; Malamuth, 1986; Muehlenhard and Linton, 1987). Muehlenhard, Friedman, and Thomas (1985) found that although most men adhered to rape-supportive attitudes to some extent, those men who scored as more traditional in their sex-role attitudes were even more likely to view rape as justifiable under three conditions: if the couple went to the man's apartment, if the woman asked the man out, or if the man paid the expenses for the date.

Rape-supportive attitudes may take the form of beliefs in rape myths. A rape myth has been defined as a "prejudicial, stereotyped or false belief about rape, rape victims, or rapists" (Burt, 1991, p. 26). Rape myths are widely accepted in our society (Burt, 1980; Check and Malamuth, 1985; Field, 1978), and more so by men than women (Check and Malamuth, 1983; Field, 1978; Malamuth and Check, 1981; Brady, Chrisler, and Hosdale, 1991; Peterson and Franzese, 1987; Quackenbush, 1991). These myths allow people to believe, for example, that a victim wanted or deserved to be assaulted, that no harm was done, or that a sexual assault never happened (Burt, 1991). In one study, the rape myth most frequently associated with sexual assault was men's belief that "no does not mean no" (Muehlenhard, Linton, Felts, and Andrews, 1985). Another male belief strongly correlated with sexual assault in this study was that violence is an acceptable response to women who "lead men on." Belief in such rape myths has been strongly correlated with men's willingness to justify rape.

Malamuth and his associates have investigated media portrayals of rape myths and the effects of these portrayals. In these studies, exposure to sexually violent depictions incorporating rape myths increased men's belief in the myths and acceptance of violence against women (Check and Malamuth, 1985; Malamuth, 1984; Malamuth and Briere, 1986; Malamuth and Ceniti, 1986; Malamuth and Check, 1981, 1985; Malamuth, Haber, and Feshbach,

1980). Men who were predisposed to be aggressive toward women were particularly susceptible to the influence of violent pornography (Malamuth and Check, 1985). Thus, exposure to sexual violence in the media can influence individuals with a proclivity to rape.

Other research has investigated the effects of rape myths on men's and women's attribution of responsibility for rape. Shotland and Goodstein (1983) found that men given a description of a hypothetical date ending in rape were more likely to blame the woman for what happened when the description depicted rape myths. Similarly, subjects who believed the more traditional sex-role stereotypes also blamed the victim more than did peers with more egalitarian attitudes (Shotland and Goodstein, 1983; Willis, 1992). Other studies indicate that men assign greater responsibility for the assault to rape victims than do women (Calhoun, Selby, and Warring, 1976; Cann, Calhoun, and Selby, 1979; Thornton and Ryckman, 1983; Kanekar and others, 1991). Also, sexual coercion is more likely when men and women differ on norms for the timing of sexual interaction, the communication of consent, and the signals of sexual interest (Burkhart and Stanton, 1988).

Personality Characteristics. The belief that rape perpetrators are psychologically disturbed individuals who differ from "normal" men has not been supported in most studies, which show that men without measurable psychological disturbance are just as likely to commit sexual assault as disturbed men. For example, Koss, Leonard, Beezley, and Oros (1988) studied sexually aggressive men and found that psychopathy did not contribute to the prediction of sexually coercive behaviors. More recent studies indicate that certain personality characteristics or childhood experiences may predispose men to be sexually aggressive without serving as indicators of overt psychopathology. Thus, men with histories of sexually coercive behavior have been found to be more hostile towards women (Koss and Dinero, 1989b), more impulsive, more involved in physical violence, and more likely to endorse force and acceptance of interpersonal violence, especially against women (Calhoun, Selby, and Warring, 1986; Malamuth, 1986; Rapaport and Burkhart, 1984). Cole (1988) found that the occurrence of coercive sex was predicted by motives for dominance, anger, hedonism, conformity, and recognition. Considerable research has also linked hypermasculine and antisocial personality characteristics with rape proclivity. This research is reviewed in more detail in the next section.

Hypermasculinity. The hypermasculine, or macho, personality has been consistently associated with sexual aggression in studies of college men. To assess this personality dimension, Mosher and Sirkin (1984) constructed the Hypermasculinity Inventory (HI), which measures callous sexual attitudes toward women and perceptions of violence as manly and danger as exciting. Mosher and Anderson (1986) found that hypermasculinity was associated with the following behaviors towards women: getting them drunk or high, treating them with anger and rejection, threatening them verbally, and using force and exploitation to get sex. In other studies, hypermasculinity has been the most consistent correlate of self-reported sexual coerciveness (Cole, 1988; Erway, 1990). The macho personality has also been related to a man's number of sexual partners, earlier age of first intercourse than other males, self-reported likelihood of raping or forcing a woman to do something against her will, and total number of consensual sexual experiences (Cole, 1988).

This personality dimension suggests extreme internalization of a socially constructed image of masculinity. Lisak (1991) notes that hypermasculinity is adopted by men who lack a model of positive, loving manhood and hypothesizes a relationship between father-distant child-rearing practices and male sexual aggression. In one study (Lisak and Roth, 1990), rapists made significantly more negative statements and significantly fewer positive statements about their fathers than control subjects, with rapists who had poor paternal relationships expressing the most hostility towards women, dominance over women, underlying motives related to power, and hypermasculine attitudes. Significantly, the rapists' maternal relationships did not correlate with any of these measures.

Such men grow up without a positive object for masculine identification and develop the hypermasculinity that Beatrice Wenting has called a "protest masculinity" (cited in Lisak, 1991, p. 259). The hypermasculine personality style provides a defense; it enables the insecurely identified male to forge an approved identity, even if it is a caricature of maleness. Lisak (1991) argues that the caricatured, hypermasculine style is encouraged and may be necessary in cultures with marked gender differentiation, where men must be "real" men and a real man is fundamentally different from a woman.

Antisocial Orientation and Socialization Deficits. Antisocial behaviors such as immaturity, irresponsibility, and lack of social conscience have been associated with coercive sexuality in studies of college men (Rapaport and Burkhart, 1984; Rapaport, 1984). Malamuth, Sockloskie, Koss, and Tanaka (1991) identified delinquency as one component of a causal model predicting coerciveness against women. Similarly, Lisak and Roth (1988) found that sexual coerciveness was associated with greater impulsivity, perceived loss of control under the influence of alcohol, willingness to discuss sexual experiences with peers, and less respect for society's rules than expressed by nonaggressive men.

In summary, hypermasculinity and low levels of socialization are key personality variables that distinguish sexually coercive from noncoercive males. The sexually coercive men overvalue being tough, unfeeling, and violent; they risk danger for excitement and minimize empathic responses. For them, sexual aggression validates and affirms their masculinity.

Sexual Styles and Early Sexual Experiences. Specific sexual styles and experiences are found among sexually coercive men. Compared to noncoercive men, they report more sexual experiences, greater dissatisfaction with their level of sexual activity, and a pattern of intensely seeking sexual outlets (Kanin, 1967). Koss and Dinero (1989a) found that male perpetrators reported earlier and more frequent childhood sexual experiences. Another line of research has examined the effects on men of women's sexual arousal during rape. In one study, exposure to portrayals of sexual arousal among victims resulted in equivalent disinhibition of arousal for both noncoercive and coercive men (Malamuth, 1986). However, Rapaport (1984) found that sexually aggressive males reported significantly more sexual arousal than nonaggressive men in response to depictions of rape, particularly if these depictions were embedded with rape myths.

Situational Factors

The predisposing factors we have described so far exist within perpetrators and may be triggered by situations that perpetrators interpret as justifying sexual intimacy. Thus, another set of risk factors for sexual assault appears in dating situation characteristics associated with male control or dominance, substance abuse, the nature of the victim–perpetrator relationship, and peer support or enabling behaviors.

Male Control and Dominance. Muehlenhard and Linton (1987) reported that men who initiated a date, paid all expenses, and provided transportation were more likely to be sexually aggressive. Engaging in these activities gives men greater power to define what happens during a date and also reflects disparities in power between men and women within society at large (Lundberg-Love and Geffner, 1989). The phenomenon of parking (engaging in intimate behavior in a car or truck), which was strongly correlated with sexual assault in one study (Muehlenhard and Linton, 1987), illustrates this dynamic. Because parking usually occurs in the man's car in an isolated place, it gives him considerably more control than his date over what happens. Similarly, other environments that increase men's control, such as fraternity houses and all-male living units, have been found to be high-risk environments for sexual assault (these environments are discussed in more detail later).

Substance Abuse. Substance use is frequently associated with sexual assaults on college campuses (Muehlenhard and Linton, 1987; Abbey, 1991; Richardson and Hammock, 1991). Koss and Dinero (1989b) found that frequent substance use was associated with the more serious incidents of sexual assault and was one of the four strongest predictors of rape among college women. Abbey (1991) suggested that alcohol increases the chances that sexual intent will be misperceived, is used to justify sexually aggressive behavior, and impairs men's and women's abilities to communicate effectively. Other studies have documented that men and women adhere to a double standard, assigning men less and women greater responsibility for sexual assaults that occur when alcohol is drunk by one or both parties (Richardson and Hammock, 1991; Norris and Cubbins, 1992). Perkins (1992) reported that approximately 25 percent of both genders experienced unwanted sex as a result of alcohol at least once within the past year, and 15 percent of the men and 10 percent of the women more than once.

Victim–Perpetrator Relationship. Perpetrators appear more likely to assault women they know than those they do not know. In one study, most incidents of sexual assault in college occurred between men and women who had known each other for at least a year (Muehlenhard and Linton, 1987). In another, 42 percent of victims had sex with the perpetrator at a later point in time (Koss, 1988). These studies contradict the belief that sexual assault is primarily perpetrated by strangers.

Close-Knit Male Peer Groups. Schaeffer and Nelson (1993) reported that college men who lived in all-male environments were more likely than other men to subscribe to rape myths. Similarly, Koss and Dinero (1989b) found a relationship between the degree of sexual assault and the perpetrator's involvement in peer groups that reinforced views of women as highly sexualized objects. Fraternities have been used as examples of the highly intensive male peer environment that reinforces rape-supportive attitudes and behaviors. Thus, Copenhaver and Grauerholz (1991) found that sorority women were at great risk of being raped in fraternity houses, and Boeringer, Shehan, and Akers (1991) reported a greater incidence of sexual assaults among fraternity members than among non-fraternity members. Martin and Hummer (1989) implicated highly intensive all-male peer groups in their analysis of fraternities and campus rape, noting the likelihood of sexual abuse in an environment that promotes stereotypical conceptions of masculinity, the use of alcohol to overcome women's sexual reluctance, and an emphasis on violence, force, and competition in relationships.

Most gang rapes that occur in college environments are perpetrated by members of such all-male groups. According to one literature review of gang rapes by college students since 1980, twenty-two of twenty-four documented cases were perpetrated by members of fraternities or intercollegiate athletic teams (O'Sullivan, 1991). Membership in such a group may "protect a perpetrator from doubts about the propriety of his behavior," especially when the group has high status and special privileges on campus (Martin and Hummer, 1989, p. 143). Participation in or observation of group sexual assault also increases group cohesiveness and resolves group members' doubts about heterosexuality, doubts that are created by physically close, intimate relationships with other men.

Misperceptions of Sexual Intent

Abbey and her colleagues have shown that college men and women interpret sexual and nonverbal cues differently, with men typically overestimating women's sexual availability and interest (Abbey, 1982, 1987, 1991; Abbey and Melby, 1986; Abbey, Cozzarelli, McLaughlin, and Harnish, 1987). Men were more likely than women to perceive male and female actors as seductive, and they were more likely to report sexual attraction toward opposite-sex targets (Abbey, 1982). These results were supported in two follow-up studies that tested variations among such stimuli as revealing target clothing, interpersonal distance, eye contact and touch, sexual composition of the dyad, and other situational cues (Abbey and Melby, 1986; Abbey, Cozzarelli, McLaughlin, and Harnish, 1987). In a related study, Shotland and Craig (1988) found that both genders make distinctions between "friendly" and "interested" behavior, but that men have a much lower threshold for the perception of sexual intent. Muehlenhard (1989) reported similar results: "No matter who initiated the date, who paid, or where the couple went, men were always more likely than women to interpret the behavior as a sign that women wanted sex" (p. 251).

In one study of actual dating experiences, perpetrators reported feeling led on, partly because they perceived their female partners to be dressed more suggestively than usual (Muehlenhard and Linton, 1987). Koss (1988) reported that men who committed a sexual assault did not define their behavior as rape, placed equal responsibility on their partners for what happened, and said they were willing to engage in similar behavior again. These perpetrators also disagreed with their victims regarding the extent to which force was used and resisted.

This research points to a considerable gender gap in men's and women's interpretations of heterosexual dating behaviors. Indeed, some researchers define cross-gender communication as a type of cross-cultural communication (Tannen, 1990). The research indicates that men are much more willing than women to interpret a variety of behaviors as indicative of sexual interest, even when the stimuli are very subtle and especially when they are ambiguous. Men see such attributes in women as friendliness, revealingness of clothing, and attractiveness as seductive while women do not see these same behaviors as seductive. Such differences in the perception of sexual intent foster misunderstanding and misinterpretation in heterosexual dating situations and may result in men's assuming that they have women's implicit consent to be intimate when no consent exists.

Implications for Rape Prevention Programs

In sum, the literature on college men's experiences as perpetrators of sexual assault, including acquaintance rape, suggests that rape is best understood as an extreme within a continuum of sexually assaultive behaviors, that sexual assault is engaged in by many men and may be somewhat normative, and that it occurs in a sociocultural environment that promotes rape-supportive attitudes and socializes men to adhere to them. In this environment, many men report engaging in unwanted sexual activity partly as a result of peer pressure to be sexually active. Figure 1.1 depicted a possible relationship among the factors that researchers have associated with men's likelihood of committing a sexual assault. The components of each factor are summarized in Table 1.1. Our review of the literature has a number of implications for the design and development of effective rape prevention programs for men. Such programs

Table 1.1. Factors Associated with Men's Increased Risk of Committing Sexual Assault

I. Perpetrator characteristics
    A. Attitudes and socialization experiences
        1. Belief in rape myths
        2. Adversarial view of gender relations
        3. Traditional gender roles
    B. Personality characteristics
        1. Hypermasculinity
            a. Hostility toward women
            b. Acceptance of violence against women
            c. Need to dominate
        2. Antisocial orientation
            a. Lack of social conscience
            b. Irresponsibility
            c. Immaturity
    C. Sexual style and early sexual experiences
        1. Earlier and more frequent sexual experiences
        2. Dissatisfaction with sexual experiences
        3. Greater sexual response to depictions of rape
II. Situational risk factors
    A. Date location and activity
    B. Man initiates and pays
    C. Alcohol and other drug use
    D. Ongoing relationship with victim
    E. Peer-group support and participation in close-knit all-male groups that emphasize the components listed under IA and IB.
    F. Dress
    G. Power differential
III. Misperception of sexual intent based on the following items
    A. Friendliness
    B. Attractiveness
    C. The situational risk factors listed above

should address the risk factors associated with men's willingness to condone or engage in sexual assault. Thus, programs should define rape and sexual assault, challenge rape myths, understand and address male socialization experiences, and gender differences in perception, and encourage men to confront peers who express adherence to rape-supportive beliefs. Because most of the variables predicting men's likelihood of committing a sexual assault are associated with men's experiences in all-male environments or with close male peers, efforts to change male attitudes and behavior may be more effective in all-male groups. In fact, rape prevention programs that focus exclusively on women may serve to reinforce the attitudes and belief systems that allow men to deny responsibility for the problem. Similarly, coed discussion groups or workshops may unintentionally reinforce differences between men and women and promote the perception of adversarial male–female relationships that is associated with men's increased proclivity to rape. In contrast, all-male workshops offer a safe environment for men to discuss the attitudes and behaviors that make them potential perpetrators and can encourage men to take action to stop rape. Peer-facilitated groups that use respected campus student leaders as role models may be particularly effective in generating positive peer pressure against rape and in modeling alternatives to traditional male sexist behavior. All-male, peer-facilitated workshop formats can also encourage men who do not adhere to rape-supportive beliefs and attitudes to speak out and have their views represented among the diversity of male viewpoints. A model program incorporating such a workshop is presented in Chapter Three.

Finally, the different degrees of rape proclivity among men indicate that different interventions are appropriate in individual cases. While current attitudes and socialization experiences make all men potential rapists who would benefit from education and prevention programs, particular men, such as those who have entrenched personality characteristics associated with rape proclivity, may need the intensive treatment approaches described in Chapter Five. The causes of sexual assault are complex and incorporate a wide range of experiences, attitudes, personality characteristics, and cognitions among men. Prevention programs are needed that will help men begin the process of self-examination and change that may ultimately reduce the incidence of rape and sexual assault on our campuses.

References

Abbey, A. "Sex Differences in Attributions for Friendly Behavior: Do Males Misperceive Females' Friendliness?" Journal of Personality and Social Psychology, 1982, 42, 830–838.

Abbey, A. "Perceptions of Personal Avoidability Versus Responsibility: How Do They Differ?" Basic and Applied Social Psychology, 1987, 8, 3–19.

Abbey, A. "Acquaintance Rape and Alcohol Consumption on College Campuses: How Are They Linked?" Journal of American College Health, 1991, 39 (4), 165–169.

Abbey, A., Cozzarelli, C., McLaughlin, K., and Harnish, R. "The Effects of Clothing and Dyad Sex Composition on Perception of Sexual Intent: Do Women and Men Evaluate These Cues Differently?" Journal of Applied Social Psychology, 1987, 17 (2), 108–126.

Abbey, A., and Melby, C. "The Effects of Nonverbal Cues on Gender Differences in Perceptions of Sexual Intent." Sex Roles, 1986, 15 (5–6), 283–298.

Aizenman, M., and Kelley, G. "The Incidence of Violence and Acquaintance Rape in Dating Relationships Among College Men and Women." Journal of College Student Development, 1988, 29, 305–311.

Baier, J., Rosenzweig, M., and Whipple, E. "Patterns of Sexual Behavior, Coercion, and Victimization of University Students." Journal of College Student Development, 1991, 32 (4), 310–322.

Berkowitz, A. D. "The Role of Coaches in Rape Prevention Programs for Athletes." In A. Parrot, N. Cummings, and T. Marchell (eds.), Rape 101: Sexual Assault Prevention for College Athletes, Holmes Beach, Fla.: Learning Publications, in press.

Berkowitz, A. "College Men as Perpetrators of Acquaintance Rape and Sexual Assault: A Review of Recent Research." Journal of American College Health, 1992, 40, 175–181.

Boeringer, S. B., Shehan, C. L., and Akers, R. L.. "Social Contexts and Social Learning in Sexual Coercion and Aggression: Assessing the Contribution of Fraternity Membership." Family Relations, 1991, 40, 58–64.

Box, S. Power, Crime and Mystification. London: Tavistock, 1983.

Brady, E. C., Chrisler, J. C., and Hosdale, D. C. "Date Rape: Expectations, Avoidance Strategies and Attitudes Toward Victims." Journal of Social Psychology, 1991, 131 (3), 427–429.

Burkhart, B. R., and Fromuth, M. E. "Individual Psychological and Social Psychological Understandings of Sexual Coercion." In E. Grauerholz and M. A. Koralewski (eds.), Sexual Coercion: A Sourcebook on Its Nature, Causes and Prevention. Lexington, Mass.: Heath, 1991.

Burkhart, B. R., and Stanton, A. "Sexual Aggression in Acquaintance Relationships." In G. W. Russell (ed.), Violence in Intimate Relationships. New York: PMA Press, 1988.

Burt, M. R. "Cultural Myths and Supports for Rape." Journal of Applied Social Psychology, 1980, 38, 217–230.

Burt, M. R. "Rape Myths and Acquaintance Rape." In A. Parrot and L. Bechhofer (eds.), Acquaintance Rape: The Hidden Crime. New York: Wiley, 1991.

Calhoun, L., Selby, J., and Warring, L. "Social Perception of the Victim's Causal Role in Rape: An Exploratory Examination of Four Factors." Human Relations, 1976, 29, 517–526.

Cann, A., Calhoun, L., and Selby, J. "Attributing Responsibility to the Victim of Rape: Influence of Information Regarding Past Sexual Experiences." Human Relations, 1979, 32, 57–67.

Check, J.V.P., and Malamuth, M. N. "Sex Role Stereotyping and Reactions to Depictions of Stranger vs. Acquaintance Rape." Journal of Personality and Social Psychology, 1983, 45, 344–356.

Check, J.V.P., and Malamuth, M. N. "An Empirical Assessment of Some Feminist Hypotheses About Rape." International Journal of Women's Studies, 1985, 8, 414–423.

Cole, J. A. "Predictors of Sexually Coercive and Aggressive Behavior in College Males." Unpublished doctoral dissertation, Auburn University, 1988.

Copenhaver, S., and Grauerholz, E. "Sexual Victimization Among Sorority Women: Exploring the Link Between Sexual Violence and Institutional Practices." Sex Roles, 1991, 24 (1–2).

David, D. S., and Brannon, R. The Forty-Nine Percent Majority. Reading, Mass.: Addison-Wesley, 1976.

Erway, L. "Comorbidity of Sexual and Physical Aggression in College Males: Toward Defining a Typology of Violence Toward Women." Unpublished doctoral dissertation, Auburn University, 1990.

Field, H. S. "Attitudes Toward Rape: A Comparative Analysis of Police, Rapists, Crisis Counselors, and Citizens." Journal of Personality and Social Psychology, 1978, 36, 156–179.

Groth, A. N. Men Who Rape. New York: Plenum, 1979.

Harney, P. A., and Muehlenhard, C. L. "Factors That Increase the Likelihood of Victimization." In A. Parrot and L. Bechhofer (eds.), Acquaintance Rape: The Hidden Crime. New York: Wiley, 1991.

Kanekar, S., Shaherwalla, A., Franco, B., Kunju, T., and Pinto, A. J. "The Acquaintance Predicament of a Rape Victim." Journal of Applied Social Psychology, 1991, 21 (18), 1524–1544.

Kanin, E. J. "Male Sex Aggression and Three Psychiatric Hypotheses." Journal of Sex Research, 1965, 1, 221–231.

Kanin, E. J. "An Examination of Sexual Aggression as a Response to Sexual Frustration." Journal of Marriage and Family, 1967, 29, 428–433.

Kanin, E. J. "Rape as a Function of Relative Sexual Frustration." Psychological Reports, 1983, 52, 133–134.

Kanin, E. J. "Date Rape: Unofficial Criminals and Victims." Victimology: An International Journal, 1984, 9, 95–108.

Kanin, E. J. "Date Rapist: Differential Sexual Socialization and Relative Deprivation." Archives of Sexual Behavior, 1985, 14, 219–230.

Koss, M. P. "Hidden Rape: Sexual Aggression and Victimization in a National Sample of Students in Higher Education." In A. W. Burgess (ed.), Rape and Sexual Assault, Vol. 2. New York: Garland, 1988.

Koss, M. P., and Dinero, T. E. "Discriminant Analysis of Risk Factors for Sexual Victimization Among a National Sample of College Women." Journal of Consulting and Clinical Psychology, 1989a, 57 (2), 242–250.

Koss, M. P., and Dinero, T. E. "Predictors of Sexual Aggression Among a National Sample of Male College Students." In R. A. Prentky and V. L. Quinsley (eds.), Human Sexual Aggression: Current Perspectives. Annals of the New York Academy of Science, 528, 133–146. New York: New York Academy of Science, 1989b.

Koss, M. P., Gidycz, C. A., and Wisniewski, N. "The Scope of Rape: Incidence and Prevalence of Sexual Aggression and Victimization in a National Sample of Higher-Education Students." Journal of Consulting and Clinical Psychology, 1987, 55, 162–170.

Koss, M. P., and Leonard, K. E. "Sexually Aggressive Men: Empirical Findings and Theoretical Implications." In N. M. Malamuth and E. Donnerstein (eds.), Pornography and Sexual Aggression. Orlando, Fla.: Academic Press, 1984, pp. 213–232.

Koss, M. P., Leonard, K. E., Beezley, D. A., and Oros, C. "Nonstranger Sexual Aggression: A Discriminant Analysis of the Psychological Characteristics of Undetected Offenders." Sex Roles, 1985, 12 (9–10), 981–992.

Lisak, D. "Sexual Aggression, Masculinity, and Fathers." Journal of Women in Culture and Society, 1991, 16 (2), 238–262.

Lisak, D., and Roth, S. "Motivational Factors in Nonincarcerated Sexually Aggressive Men." Journal of Personality and Social Psychology, 1988, 55, 795–802.

Lisak, D., and Roth, S. "Motives and Psychodynamics of Self-Reported, Unincarcerated Rapists." American Journal of Orthopsychiatry, 1990, 60 (2), 268–280.

Lundberg-Love, P., and Geffner, R. "Date Rape: Prevalence, Risk Factors and a Proposed Model." In M. A. Pirog-Good and J. E. Stets (eds.), Violence in Dating Relationships: Emerging Social Issues. New York: Praeger, 1989.

Malamuth, N. M. "Aggression Against Women: Cultural and Individual Causes." In N. M. Malamuth and E. Donnerstein (eds.), Pornography and Sexual Aggression. San Diego: Academic Press, 1984.

Malamuth, N. M. "Predictors of Naturalistic Sexual Aggression." Journal of Personality and Social Psychology, 1986, 50, 953–962.

Malamuth, N. M., and Briere, J. "Sexual Violence in the Media: Indirect Effects on Aggression Against Women." Journal of Social Issues, 1986, 42, 75–92.

Malamuth, N. M., and Ceniti, J. "Repeated Exposure to Violent and Nonviolent Pornography: Likelihood of Raping Ratings and Laboratory Aggression Against Women." Aggressive Behavior, 1986, 12, 129–137.

Malamuth, N. M., and Check, J.V.P. "The Effects of Mass Media Exposure on Acceptance of Violence Against Women: A Field Experiment." Journal of Research in Personality, 1981, 15, 436–446.

Malamuth, N. M., and Check, J.V.P. "The Effects of Aggressive Pornography on Beliefs in Rape Myths: Individual Differences." Journal of Research in Personality, 1985, 19, 299–320.

Malamuth, N. M., Haber, S., and Feshbach, S. "Testing Hypotheses Regarding Rape: Exposure to Sexual Violence, Sex Differences, and the 'Normality' of Rapists." Journal of Research in Personality, 1980, 14, 121–137.

Malamuth, N. M., Sockloskie, R. J., Koss, M. P., and Tanaka, J. S. "Characteristics of Aggressors Against Women: Testing a Model Using a National Sample of College Students." Journal of Consulting and Clinical Psychology, 1991, 59 (5), 670–681.

Mandoki, C. A., and Burkhart, B. R. "Women as Victims: Antecedents and Consequences of Acquaintance Rape." In A. Parrot and L. Bechhofer (eds.), Acquaintance Rape: The Hidden Crime. New York: Wiley, 1991.

Margolin, L., Miller, M., and Moran, P. B. "When a Kiss Is Not Just a Kiss: Relating Violations of Consent in Kissing to Rape Myth Acceptance." Sex Roles, 1989, 20 (5–6), 231–243.

Martin, P. Y., and Hummer, R. A. "Fraternities and Rape on Campus." Gender and Society, 1989, 3 (4), 457–473.

Mosher, D. L., and Anderson, R. D. "Macho Personality, Sexual Aggression, and Reactions to Guided Imagery of Realistic Rape." Journal of Research in Personality, 1986, 20, 77–94.

Mosher, D. L., and Sirkin, M. "Measuring a Macho Personality Constellation." Journal of Research in Personality, 1984, 18, 150–163.

Muehlenhard, C. L. "Misinterpreted Dating Behaviors and the Risk of Date Rape." In M. A. Pirog-Good and J. E. Stets (eds.), Violence in Dating Relationships: Emerging Social Issues. New York: Praeger, 1989.

Muehlenhard, C. L., and Cook, S. W. "Men's Reports of Unwanted Sexual Activity." Journal of Sex Research, 1988, 24, 58–72.

Muehlenhard, C. L., Friedman, D. E., and Thomas, C. M. "Is Date Rape Justifiable? The Effects of Dating Activity, Who Initiated, Who Paid, and Men's Attitudes Towards Women." Psychology of Women Quarterly, 1985, 9 (3), 297–310.

Muehlenhard, C. L., and Linton, M. A. "Date Rape and Sexual Aggression in Dating Situations: Incidence and Risk Factors." Journal of Counseling Psychology, 1987, 34 (2), 186–196.

Muehlenhard, C. L., Linton, M. A., Felts, A. S., and Andrews, S. L. "Men's Attitudes Toward the Justifiability of Date Rape: Intervening Variables and Possible Solutions." Paper presented at the session "Sexual Coercion: Political Issues and Empirical Findings," E. R. Allgeier (chair), at the Midcontinent meeting of the Society for the Scientific Study of Sex, Chicago, 1985.

Norris, J., and Cubbins, L. A. "Eating, Drinking, and Rape." Psychology of Women Quarterly, 1992, 16, 179–191.

O'Neil, J. "Assessing Men's Gender Role Conflict." In D. Moore and F. Leafgreen (eds.), Problem Solving Strategies and Interventions for Men in Conflict. Alexandria, Va.: American Association for Counseling and Development, 1990.

O'Sullivan, C. S. "Acquaintance Gang Rape on Campus." In A. Parrot and L. Bechhofer (eds.), Acquaintance Rape: The Hidden Crime. New York: Wiley, 1991.

Parrot, A., and Bechhofer, L. (eds.). Acquaintance Rape: The Hidden Crime. New York: Wiley, 1991.

Perkins, H. W. "Gender Patterns in Consequences of Collegiate Alcohol Abuse: A Ten Year Study of Trends in an Undergraduate Population." Journal of Studies on Alcohol, 1992, 53 (5), 458–462.

Peterson, S. A., and Franzese, B. "Correlates of College Men's Sexual Abuse of Women." Journal of College Student Development, 1987, 28, 223–228.

Quackenbush, R. "Attitudes of College Men Toward Women and Rape." Journal of College Student Development, 1991, 32, 376–377.

Rapaport, K. "Sexually Aggressive Males: Characterological Features and Sexual Responsiveness to Rape Depictions." Unpublished doctoral dissertation, Auburn University, 1984.

Rapaport, K., and Burkhart, B. R. "Personality and Attitudinal Characteristics of Sexually Coercive College Males." Journal of Abnormal Psychology, 1984, 93 (2), 216–221.

Reilly, M. E., Lott, B., Caldwell, D., and DeLuca, L. "Tolerance for Sexual Harassment Related to Self-Reported Sexual Victimization." Gender and Society, 1991, 6 (1), 122–138.

Richardson, D., and Hammock, G. S. "Alcohol and Acquaintance Rape." In A. Parrot and L. Bechhofer (eds.), Acquaintance Rape: The Hidden Crime. New York: Wiley, 1991.

Schaeffer, A. M., and Nelson, E. S. "Rape-Supportive Attitudes: Effects of On-Campus Residence and Education." Journal of College Student Development, 1993, 34, 175–179.

Shotland, L., and Craig, J. "Can Men and Women Differentiate Between Friendly and Sexually Interested Behavior?" Social Psychology Quarterly, 1988, 51 (1), 66–73.

Shotland, L., and Goodstein, L. "Just Because She Doesn't Want to Doesn't Mean It's Rape: An Experimentally Based Causal Model of the Perception of Rape in a Dating Situation." Social Psychology Quarterly, 1983, 46, 220–232.

Skelton, C. A. "Situational and Personological Correlates of Sexual Victimization in College Women." Unpublished doctoral dissertation, Auburn University, 1982.

Tannen, D. *You Just Don't Understand: Women and Men in Conversation.* New York: Ballantine Books, 1990.

Thornton, B., and Ryckman, R. M. "The Influence of a Rape Victim's Physical Attractiveness on Observers' Attributions of Responsibility." *Human Relations,* 1983, *36,* 549–562.

West, D. J., Roy, C., and Nichols, F. L. *Understanding Sexual Attacks.* London: Heinemann, 1978.

Williams, J. E., and Holmes, K. A. *The Second Assault: Rape and Public Attitudes.* Westport, Conn.: Greenwood, 1981.

Willis, C. E. "The Effect of Sex Role Stereotype, Victim and Defendant Race, and Prior Relationship on Rape Culpability Attributions." *Sex Roles,* 1992, *26* (5–6), 213–226.

ALAN D. BERKOWITZ is counseling center director and assistant professor of psychology at Hobart and William Smith Colleges.

BARRY R. BURKHART is professor of psychology at Auburn University.

SUSAN E. BOURG is a graduate student in clinical psychology at Auburn University.

Rape prevention in the context of a problematic masculinity is discussed; conservative, mythopoetic, and feminist perspectives on masculinity are reviewed; and a feminist foundation for rape prevention programs for men is proposed.

Disconnected Lives: Men, Masculinity, and Rape Prevention

Rocco L. Capraro

Speaking in a nationally televised panel discussion on rape and men, F. Lee Bailey articulated what he saw as a recent paradigm shift in our understanding of rape: we used to think of rape as something that happens "in the man's mind." We now think of rape as something that happens "in the woman's mind" (Jennings, 1992). While Bailey may be better known as a defense attorney than as a theorist about rape, his peculiar and unsettling comment marked an important moment in the panel's dialogue and in our contemporary discussion on rape. What Bailey meant was that, when discourse about rape centered on the issue of *force*, the perpetrator's state of mind, *his* intentionality, was critical to our interpretation of rape. But as discourse about rape came to center on the issue of *consent*, the victim's state of mind, *her* intentionality, became critical to our interpretation of rape. We are, rightly, coming to understand rape as a female experience, largely as a result of listening to women's voices, particularly those that tell us about women's victimization in acquaintance rape. We are coming to know victimization in rape as a specific female experience (Brownmiller, 1975; Estrich, 1987; Warshaw, 1988; Donat and D'Emilio, 1992; White and Sorenson, 1992; Beneke, 1982).

Still, it is men who rape. An understanding of the female experience of victimization, by itself, will not prevent one rape. Until men come to know themselves as perpetrators, that is, until men experience their perpetration as perpetration, we can have little hope for change. Rape prevention education that addresses men as the perpetrators of rape must come full circle, back to men and back to male experience, this time to know *perpetration* of rape as a specific *male experience.*

In this chapter, I argue that our understanding of the specific act of rape should be embedded in our understanding of masculinity. Rape is not an isolated behavior, but a behavior linked in men's lives to larger systems of attitudes, values, and modalities of conduct that constitute masculinity. In this model, rape prevention work begins with men and with men's questioning of prevailing assumptions about masculinity and their rethinking what it means to be a man. I am extremely skeptical of any rape prevention work that proposes solutions to the problem of rape but leaves masculinity, as we know it today, largely intact.

In the last decade, writers from a variety of perspectives have offered general theories of masculinity and corresponding programs for personal and social change in men (Clatterbaugh, 1990). In the following sections, I explore three important perspectives on masculinity—conservative, mythopoetic, and feminist—and their potential for changing men's attitudes. I conclude that the feminist perspective is most likely to bring about changes in men's concept of masculinity that will result in effective rape prevention, and that rape prevention work with men should, therefore, be undertaken from a feminist perspective.

Masculinity and Male Subjectivity

Why would a man rape, penetrate a woman, without her consent? Research on college men as perpetrators (reviewed in Chapter One) suggests that most college men who commit acquaintance rape would not define their behavior as rape. Rapists are unwilling or unable to label their actions correctly. The model of sexual assault Berkowitz, Burkhart, and Bourg propose in Chapter One identifies two critical factors that obstruct men's views of their own inappropriate behavior: perpetrator characteristics (male socialization, attitudes, personality characteristics, and early sexual experiences) and situational risks (possession of control and dominance, use of alcohol and other drugs, and membership in male peer groups). The model answers the question: the perpetration of rape is traceable to a highly problematic masculinity, constituted by sexism, violence, and homophobia (Berkowitz, 1992). In short, the perpetration of rape is not about the woman but about the man and about socialized ways of being a man, in a profound sense. When men rape, they are being men (Stoltenberg, 1989).

Consider the extreme case of a fraternity gang rape. Peggy Sanday documents the gruesome objectification of the female victim that occurs as an intersubjective bond is constructed among the male perpetrators (Sanday, 1990). At the risk of further objectifying the victim, we can interpret Sanday's findings to mean that a fraternity gang rape, in the perpetrators' minds, is more about the ways men want to act with each other than it is about the ways they want to act with the victim. The victim becomes a means to the perpetrators' ends, which are entangled in the teleology of their masculinity.

The Spur Posse group of high school boys in Lakewood, California, and the "whirlpool" phenomenon at public swimming pools in New York City are other examples of sexual assault on girls and women in the service of inter-subjective, masculine bonding. Spur Posse members competed with each other by scoring points "each time they achieved orgasm with a different girl" (Smolowe, 1993, p. 41). The whirlpool was a method of sexual assault "in which young men wrapped arms and churned through the water, ripping the bathing suits off young girls and fondling them" (McLarin, 1993, p. B3). These occurrences dramatize the concept that a man's sexual assault of a woman can be a bond that forges links between the perpetrator and other men, literally present or not, and with masculinity itself.

Object relations theory provides a useful framework for understanding male intersubjectivity. In Jessica Benjamin's account of intersubjectivity (1988), the self develops an awareness of its distinctions from others through a process of differentiation that occurs between the poles of assertion and recognition. Assertion entails the declaration, "I am, I do." Recognition entails the response, "you are, you have done," and recognition assumes many forms: "to recognize is to affirm, validate, acknowledge, know, accept, understand, empathize, take in, tolerate, appreciate, see, identify with, find familiar, . . . love." Intersubjectivity occurs when one subject recognizes another subject "as different, yet alike, as an other who is capable of showing similar mental experience" (pp. 11–25). In my view, masculinity itself can be seen as a kind of male inter-subjectivity that develops as men assert themselves and recognize each other in a context of shared meaning and experience as men and fail to recognize or empathize with women.

Rape prevention programs may respond to the various components of the sexual assault model (by addressing men's attitudes toward women, for exam-ple, or providing alcohol awareness education), but rape prevention education for men will bring about the greatest change only when men themselves begin to question prevailing models of masculinity and redefine, in practice and the-ory, what it means to be a man. Insofar as masculinity shapes, and is shaped by, male experience, transforming masculinity will change the way men live in the world, the way men know and experience the world. Transforming mas-culinity will change the way male consciousness confronts the phenomeno-logical world and will change male intersubjectivity—the shaping of the male self (Arendell, 1992).

Identifying the transformation of masculinity as a goal in rape prevention strategy raises important questions about masculinity itself. Just what are we talking about changing when we say we want to transform masculinity? Is mas-culinity changeable? And if so, how?

Meanings of Masculinity

Masculinity carries various meanings. In one sociological formulation, mas-culinity is what men are (social reality), what we think men are (stereotype), and what we would like men to be (gender role) (Clatterbaugh, 1990). In a neopsychoanalytic formulation, masculinity is an identity acquired in the object relations of early family life when a boy detaches from the mother and identifies with the father and begins the shaping of a male self (Chodorow, 1979; Butler, 1990; Benjamin, 1988; Silverman, 1992). In a political formulation, masculinity is a discourse of power, a linguistic strategy that perpetuates the domination of women by men (Brittan, 1989; Hearn, 1987; Scott, 1988).

All these meanings share an understanding of masculinity as a description of difference between men's and women's lives or as a description of the uniqueness of male experience. Thus, the concept of masculinity leads us to recognize that to be a man or a woman, to be gendered, is to experience the world in different ways (a different subjectivity) and to have different experiences in the world (a different objectivity). Masculinity is the name for the totality of difference in men's lives (Capraro, 1991).

Provisionally, then, masculinity as a description of difference has three components: "true sex" (the male body found in nature), "discrete gender" (the cultural meanings that the sexual body assumes), and "specific sexuality" (sexual object choice) (Butler, 1990, p. 128). The classic distinction between sex and gender stipulates that sex is about the body and gender is about the cultural formations around the body. While the male body is a universal found in nature, men as gendered beings are socially constructed and, therefore, historically variable. In this model, masculinity is mutable at its origins in some new staging of Oedipal drama or in male development and socialization during men's life course in society (Brod, 1987; Kimmel and Messner, 1989; Rotundo, 1993).

Three Perspectives on Masculinity

Over the past ten years, several specific perspectives on masculinity have emerged, advancing both theories of masculinity and personal and social change programs that promise solutions to the general problem of masculinity and, by inference, to the specific problem of rape (Clatterbaugh, 1990). My discussion here focuses on the three perspectives that are the leading contenders for changing men: conservative, mythopoetic, and feminist.

Conservative Perspective. The conservative perspective on masculinity represents a contemporary statement of so-called traditional U.S. values. "At the core of conservatism is a defense of the traditional gender roles whereby the masculine role of protector and provider is appropriate to men and the feminine role of childbearer and caregiver is appropriate to women" (Clatterbaugh, 1990, p. 15).

To moral and biological conservatives, men are naturally and necessarily dominant. In Men and Marriage, a classic text in the conservative perspective on masculinity, George Gilder (1986) describes men as "barbarians" who must be "tamed" by women who create "civilization" by "transforming male lust into love." Left unattached to family, which Gilder defines as mother and child, men will lead violent, anomic lives. Installing men at the head of the "traditional family" gives men something positive to do (being good providers and fathers) and protects society from men who would otherwise wander as barbarians, perpetrating rape and other atrocities (pp. 1–18, 39–47). Gilder's pessimism about male nature is essentialist. Biological imperatives determine male behavior, and "biology, anthropology, and history all tell the same story. Every society, each generation, faces an invasion by barbarians. They storm into the streets and schools, businesses and households of the land, and unless brought to heel, they rape and pillage, debauch and despoil the settlements of society. These barbarians are young men and boys, in their teens and early twenties" (p. 39).

For Gilder and other conservatives, rape is one outcome of the failure to civilize men, that is, to connect men properly to the family. Feminism, the welfare state, individualism, and a variety of other developments of liberalism are responsible for a problematic masculinity. They sanction a detachment of men from families that allows men to embark on what the feminist Barbara Ehrenreich (1983) once characterized as a "flight from commitment," and that provides women and children with support structures that make men superfluous. Life can continue without them. Single men are "peripheral men," who become rapists, drug addicts, and playboys (Gilder, 1986, pp. 61–68).

Mythopoetic Perspective. Robert Bly is the central voice of the mythopoetic perspective. In "What Men Really Want," a classic interview with Keith Thompson (Thompson, 1982), Bly asserted that recent concepts of masculinity have generated two unacceptable models of what it means to be a man. Both are corruptions of an ancient "male mode of feeling." Bly identifies these models as the '50s male, who represents the "traditional" man as father and breadwinner, and the "soft" male, who has found his feminine side through encounters with the feminist movement. The '50s male "didn't see women's souls very well, though he looked at their bodies a lot." The '50s male is capable of multiple kinds of violence—against women, against his fellow men, and against the earth. The soft male is weak and unassertive and lacks the "fierceness" necessary to confront his enemies (pp. 31–32). Neither the '50s male nor the soft male is acceptable to Bly. The '50s male is violent, the soft male simply unhappy.

Bly recounts the story of a lost masculinity or "male psyche," buried deep within the individual, beneath layers of modern, industrial society, and of men's longing to find this psyche (Thompson, 1982, p. 34). The factory, the office building, and other dislocations of labor in the modern world have removed fathers from the shop and the farm, separating boys from their fathers and other men. Boys no longer work beside their fathers, absorbing their teachings about work and life and learning what it means to be a man. Instead, boys are placed in the hands of their mothers and other women. The absence of fathers and other adult males in their lives means boys search elsewhere for models of masculinity. The presence of mothers and other adult females means boys grow up under the domination of women and with imperatives to please them. Thus, boys grow up deprived of their masculinity, and this deprivation causes a sense of "grief" among men, a sense of themselves as "wounded" (Thompson, 1982, pp. 33, 51).

Bly's remedy for this problematic modern masculinity is men's recovery of the masculinity that lies buried within them (going down is the image he uses to describe men's journey to masculinity). Mythopoetic texts—fairy tales, legends, myths, and hearth stories—in so far as they are uncorrupted by modernity, "amount to a reservoir" of truth about masculinity and ways of recovering it. Iron John, Bly's best-selling book (1990), is an elaborate exegesis of one such myth. Iron John is the Wild Man, or Hairy Man, who lives at the bottom of a swamp in the forest and represents the "psyche of primitive man" (Bly, 1990, pp. xi, 6). According to Bly, contemporary man may solve the problem of masculinity by first "bucketing-out his psyche to find the ancient hairy man under the water of his soul" and then undergoing an initiation ritual through "the active intervention of older men which is a kind of second birth, this time a birth from men" (Bly, 1990, p. 6, 15–16). The men's gatherings to discover masculinity, reported in our national press, are the site of these initiations.

Feminist Perspective. To feminists, men as a group have power over women as a group. Sexism is the foundation of gender differences, that is, differences in the male and female experience. Men are socialized to stigmatize and devalue women or anything feminine. "Labeling women deviant" allows men to control women through sexist practices and violence, including sexual harassment and rape (Schur, 1984). The devaluation of women contributes to homophobia, which, in one formulation, represents "the fear of being turned into a woman" (Kupers, 1993, pp. 45–57). Sexism also hurts men themselves. Harry Brod suggests that the interests advanced for men in a sexist society "are interests men would in some meaningful sense be better off without. . . . The material rewards conferred on men as group by patriarchy . . . come at too high a personal cost. Male sex roles are damaging to men" (Brod, 1987, pp. 54–58). What Brod has in mind are such features of male experience as high rates of health problems, alcoholism, criminal incarceration, and suicide; restricted emotional lives; and alienated sexuality.

The feminist solution to problematic masculinity is the sharing of power by men and women (liberal feminists) or the complete dismantling of male power (radical feminists). Ending sexism and achieving a gender-just society will remove the vulnerability of women as women and will also allow men to overcome the alienation intrinsic in their role as oppressors.

Disconnected Lives

Although there are significant differences among these three perspectives, they have in common the message that men today live disconnected lives and that this disconnection is the origin of their problematic masculinity. The three perspectives also share the message that reconnecting men's lives will rehabilitate masculinity. For the conservatives, liberalism, including feminism and the welfare state, has disconnected men from the traditional family by making men superfluous. The conservative solution is to resist liberal change and to reconnect men to the traditional family, as family head. For those who advance a mythopoetic view, advancing industrialism has disconnected men from other men by removing fathers from boys' lives. The mythopoetic solution is to recover a buried masculinity, which lies beneath the layers of recent human history, by reconnecting men to other men in ritual initiations. For the feminists, a worldwide, historical system of male supremacy and gender oppression has disconnected men from women by instituting male power. The feminist solution is to dismantle male power and its masculinity oppressive to women by reconnecting men to women.

Each of the three perspectives also has a theory of the male self and a politics. Conservatives argue that any male self is rooted in biology, and the best a society can do is to put more restraints on that self through a civilizing process of values and scripted gender roles. Conservatives are also politically conservative and pragmatic. Competition and survival of the fittest will determine the appropriate politics (Clatterbaugh, 1990). Those who view the self mythopoetically see the self as innate. Theirs is a self-help program that brings a man back to a lost self. They tend to describe themselves as apolitical and seek personal solutions to problems that may have political origins. (This, of course, is a political stance.) bell hooks (1992) argues that the mythopoetic "focus on personal self-actualization" contributes to the "depoliticization of the struggle to end sexism and sexist oppression" (p. 113). Feminists understand the self to be socially constructed under various political, social, and economic regimes. Changing the male self is possible through changing the concepts of masculinity and the structures that shape selves. For this reason, the feminist perspective on masculinity carries with it a politics of change; for feminists, the personal is explicitly political.

A Feminist Foundation for Rape Prevention

Which of these perspectives should serve as a foundation for programs most likely to generate change in men and result in effective rape prevention? In the past several years of teaching courses on men and masculinity to men ranging in age from seventeen to seventy, I have observed the following. The conservative perspective speaks to most men ideologically. Most men want some version of the traditional family to work, even if they recognize that it may not be working for many in contemporary society. The mythopoetic perspective speaks to most men emotionally. Bly brings out tears of grief in men of all ages and not simply because he is a brilliant poet. From the point of view of emotional needs, Bly has identified the state of many men today. The feminist perspective, however, speaks to what men need to become to resolve a problematic masculinity. In my view, most of the problems articulated in any of the three perspectives are traceable to sexism. Feminism provides the most coherent account of male experience. Thus, I argue for the feminist perspective as the foundation of rape prevention work with men.

Clatterbaugh (1990) has analyzed some of the flaws and contradictions in the conservative perspective. In general, it relies on nature and biology to justify its arguments and practices, but when what is natural is not consistent with conservatism's worldview, the conservative perspective invokes culture and values to improve upon nature (p. 30). In addition, Gilder and other conservatives virtually ignore such realities as domestic violence, marital rape, and child abuse, and the actuality that "the traditional family is hardly a safe and secure place for women" (Clatterbaugh, 1990, p. 31). Conservatives tend to argue, tautologically, that harmful elements within families—domestic violence, for example—indicate that the traditional family is simply not present or functioning. In short, the conservative dichotomy of the married man and the unmarried man does not contain a coherent account of sexual assault and male violence. Connecting all men to family is no guarantee that rape will disappear.

Others have criticized Bly and the mythopoetic perspective, saying, for example, that "Bly romanticizes history, trivializes sexist oppression, and lays the blame for men's 'grief' on women" (Pelka, 1991, p. 17). Bly has virtually no data to support any of his claims. What evidence is there that Iron John does not rape? Bly is a poet, and his poetry about his subjective experience in the world resonates in the lives of many other men. For Bly, the responses from the men he encounters are evidence enough of the truth of his claims, but what concerns me most about Bly's perspective is that many men may be responding to the antifeminine or antifeminist components of his thought (Faludi, 1991). The same reservation applies to Gilder and other conservatives. Susan Faludi (1991) observes a "powerful counter-assault on women's rights" (p. xviii) which she characterizes as a backlash that blames feminism itself for a variety of social problems faced by women. Bly and Gilder are important figures in the "backlash brain trust" that specializes in antifeminist polemic (p. 281).

It would be curious, indeed, and counterintuitive, to ground rape prevention in an antifeminist perspective, whether it be conservative or mythopoetic. Ultimately, I find myself arguing for the feminist perspective on feminist grounds. Rape prevention work is inherently feminist.

Response to Feminist Perspective Critics. Critics of the feminist perspective will be skeptical of any feminist approach to rape prevention. Men, they will say, need more culture not less. Women need more prudence and self-restraint. Camille Paglia (1992) insists that "feminism has put young women in danger by hiding the truth about sex from them." Sex is dangerous and can never be anything but dangerous. "Aggression and eroticism are deeply intertwined" in male sexuality. There is no trusting men when it comes to sex. A woman "must take responsibility for her sexuality, which is nature's red flame.

She must be prudent and cautious about where she goes and with whom." Paglia's "solution to date rape" is "female self-awareness and self-control" (pp. 49–54). Faludi (1991) regards Paglia as another servant to the backlash against women and feminism. While Paglia warns women to look out for themselves, Katie Roiphe (1993a) worries that "rape-crisis feminism" is reactionary and may actually be reconstituting the 1950s "ideal" of an innocent woman who needs to be protected by a virtuous man and vigilant social institutions. New definitions of rape founded on new models of consent do not hold women responsible for their choices and actions and assume women are "helpless and naive." For Roiphe, sex without consent "isn't necessarily always the man's fault" (pp. 27–29, 40, 68).

While claiming a place within feminism for themselves, Paglia and Roiphe have close links to the conservative perspective on masculinity in their views on the nature of sex and the role of culture. They ultimately blame women for rape, suggesting that, since there is little society can do about men, it is up to women to take control of their own lives. Their solution to the problem of rape is to change the victim, not the perpetrator. This view makes women who are raped exceptions to the rule: most women are not raped so there must be something wrong with those who are (Roiphe, 1993b, p. 68). This is the very differentiation and stigmatization of the victim that William Ryan articulates in his classic text, Blaming the Victim (1976).

Ryan (1976) argues that to blame the victim is to say that the victim "contains within himself [or herself] the causes" of the problem. This leads us to ask, "What is wrong with the victim?" Those who blame the victim usually express "a deep concern" for the victim on humanitarian grounds and attribute the problem to "environmental causation." Thus, they have it both ways—they can express concern for the victim and "condemn the vague stresses that produced the defect" but also "ignore the continuing effect of victimizing social forces." Once blame is located in the victim, the "formula for action becomes extraordinarily simple: change the victim" (pp. 1–18). Ryan's point is that blaming the victim does not solve problems. When Paglia, Roiphe, and others blame the women victims of rape for the problem of rape, they are, in effect, accepting the status quo for men and masculinity.

Rape prevention requires universalistic not exceptionalistic strategies. Universalistic strategies address the source of the problem and not simply the victim of the problem. Exceptionalistic strategies offer only some support for the victim, no long-term solution to the problem (Ryan, 1976, p. 17). Even rape prevention education workshops for women, while prudential, may be a version of blaming the victim in so far as they address victims rather than perpetrators. Working with men from a feminist perspective gets to the problem at its source.

Feminism in Men's Lives. College men tend to resist the feminist perspective. Just at the moment when the manhood many college men have been socialized to claim is seemingly within their grasp, the feminist perspective boldly challenges their assumptions about what it means to be a man and asks these men to think against themselves. In a model of "the change process for men," Ronald May (1988, p. 13) explains the stages men go through as they develop a feminist or antisexist consciousness. The first stage, "preawareness," finds men accepting an "oppressor" role. The second stage, "awakening," finds men beginning to acknowledge the reality of sexist oppression. In the third stage, men "experience a high level of emotional involvement in challenging traditional roles." At this developmental stage, they "experience guilt toward their own sexist attitudes and behaviors." May advises that "open discussion formats in same-sex groups facilitate the expression of personal feelings" and therefore promote male development at this stage. In the fourth and final stage, men "review, reflect, and integrate" their consciousness of sexism into their lives. May urges that, at this stage, "men need to bond with other men in examining male roles" but also need to connect with women in support of "the rights of men and women." May therefore recommends combining same-sex and mixed-sex sessions in educational programs and group work. (The student experiences recounted in Chapter Four are consistent with May's model.)

Rape prevention work with men should begin where they are in their needs and development and then move toward a feminist critique of masculinity. College men are confused and anxious about being men. At Hobart College, where I teach, rape prevention workshops for men begin by asking, "What is difficult about being a man?" One response is nearly universal: social pressure. When I ask men in Elderhostel (an educational program for men and women aged sixty and older) the same question, one response is also nearly universal: responsibility. Men feel pressure to perform as men. An all-male group exploration of that pressure should launch rape prevention work. Such an exploration will also illuminate men's resistance to feminism and help workshop facilitators understand men's uneasiness around feminism. It would seem that men's resistance to feminism is in the men and not in the feminism.

How do men get from where they are to where they need to be? Again, programs must begin with men's experience and feelings and then introduce the paradigms that form the context for the experience and feelings and give them meaning. While the conservative and mythopoetic perspectives begin with men's experience and feelings, they move too quickly to validate men's anger or blaming of women, leaving men fundamentally unchanged. Feminism contains within itself a pedagogy that can carry men from their experience to solutions to the problems of masculinity.

Victor Seidler (1990) writes powerfully about men's response to feminism, noting that, too often, "the response of men to feminism has been a negation by men of their own masculinity." In feminism, "masculinity was taken to be essentially oppressive to women and as being a structure of oppression." Many men coming into contact with feminism or identifying with feminism have come to understand "masculinity as essentially a relationship of power" and, in "guilt and self denial," have simply rejected their own masculinity as they sought reconciliation with women. Other men have reacted to feminism with "a kind of anti-feminist politics" (pp. 216–217). Neither, says Seidler, is an appropriate response to "the challenges of feminism" (p. 218). When we are men, we cannot simply "cut out or eradicate those parts of ourselves, of our feelings and desires, that we judge as wanting" (p. 220). Theories about the social construction of gender should not be taken so literally as to assume that nature is always strictly under the control of culture and that culture is always strictly under the control of reason.

Rather, the challenge of feminism is for men to engage in a dialogue that brings together male experience and a critique of masculinity. Feminism asks men to explore their own experience and to develop a new language for talking about that experience, a language that is neither the rational grid of male reason nor the rational grid of feminist analysis. For Seidler, feminism asks men to understand that there is a "dialectic between experience and identity," between men's lives and their masculinity. Entering this dialectic will empower men to shape a different history. Ultimately, feminism insists that men "take responsibility for their masculinity" (p. 226).

Feminism empowers men in two ways. It asks them to work for the reform of structures that perpetuate the oppression of women and are harmful to men themselves, and to take responsibility in their own lives. The writings of John Stoltenberg (1989) are a good representation of the dual empowerment that Seidler envisions. "Refusing to be a man" is Stoltenberg's way of taking responsibility for his own actions and of demystifying masculinity so it is seen as a relation of power, not a given thing. Stoltenberg argues that gender identity is "an idea" or a fiction that "has a claim on us that our actual experience does not; for if our experience 'contradicts' it, we will bend our experience so that it will make sense in terms of the idea." Gender identity carries its own moral framework for behavior. It declares that "some things are wrong for a woman to do while right for a man and other things are wrong for a man to do while right for a woman." The fiction of gender identity permits the construction of a "rapist ethics" that ascribes good and bad, right and wrong according to gender identity. Once men acknowledge this fiction, they have the knowledge to change how they act (pp. 9–24). Both Seidler and Stoltenberg ask men to move through their problematic socialized masculinity, to their actual, lived experience and to a humanist, not a masculine, ethics.

Stoltenberg's essay "Other Men" (in Stoltenberg, 1989) documents the existential drama and isolation of an antisexist man who confronts sexism in his own life and in the lives of his fellow men—the very men he depends on for affirmation of his own masculinity or male identity. Male intersubjectivity relentlessly works on the man to feel and behave the way masculinity dictates, but breaking free of the control of masculinity is a kind of catharsis. Men who do break free become free in their personal relationships and empowered to pursue a variety of activist issues, such as rape prevention or efforts against pornography, in order to reform structures that perpetuate fictions of gender identity and male supremacy.

Rape prevention education for men from a feminist perspective seeks to raise men's consciousness of their own masculinity and insists that men take responsibility for their own behavior. Men should neither deny nor accept their masculinity; rather, they should confront and understand it. In the light of our paradigm shift toward understanding women's experience of victimization in rape, "rape" and "sex" may begin to "look a lot alike" (Roiphe, 1993a, p. 40). Rape prevention education programs for men based on a feminist perspective ask men to explore this kind of ambiguity in the context of their identity and their experience, that is, in the context of their masculinity. They may then come to know a rape as a rape and be in a position to prevent rape.

References

Arendell, T. "The Social Self as Gendered: A Masculinist Discourse of Divorce." Symbolic Interaction, 1992, 15 (2), 151–181.

Beneke, T. Men on Rape: What They Have to Say About Sexual Violence. New York: St. Martin's Press, 1982.

Benjamin, J. The Bonds of Love: Psychoanalysis, Feminism, and the Problem of Domination. New York: Pantheon Books, 1988.

Berkowitz, A. "College Men as Perpetrators of Acquaintance Rape and Sexual Assault: A Review of Recent Research." Journal of American College Health, 1992, 40, 175–181.

Bly, R. Iron John: A Book About Men. Reading, Mass.: Addison-Wesley, 1990.

Brittan, A. Masculinity and Power. New York: Basil Blackwell, 1989.

Brod, H. "The Case for Men's Studies." In H. Brod (ed.), The Making of Masculinities: The New Men's Studies. Boston: Allen & Unwin, 1987.

Brownmiller, S. Against Our Will: Men, Women and Rape. New York: Bantam, 1975.

Butler, J. Gender Trouble: Feminism and the Subversion of Identity. New York: Routledge, 1990.

Capraro, R. L. "Difference, Experience, Power: Gender Awareness and Feminist Pedagogy." Paper delivered at Colgate University, Mar. 1991.

Chodorow, N. The Reproduction of Mothering: Psychoanalysis and the Sociology of Gender. Berkeley: University of California Press, 1979.

Clatterbaugh, K. Contemporary Perspectives on Masculinity: Men, Women, and Politics in Modern Society. Boulder, Colo.: Westview Press, 1990.

Donat, P.L.N., and D'Emilio, J. "A Feminist Redefinition of Rape and Sexual Assault: Historical Foundation and Change." Journal of Social Issues, 1992, 48 (1), 9–22.

Ehrenreich, B. The Hearts of Men: American Dreams and the Flight from Commitment. New York: Anchor/Doubleday, 1983.

Estrich, S. Real Rape: How the Legal System Victimizes Women Who Say No. Cambridge, Mass.: Harvard University Press, 1987.

Faludi, S. Backlash: The Undeclared War Against American Women. New York: Anchor/Doubleday, 1991.

Gilder, G. Men and Marriage. Gretna, La.: Pelican, 1986.

Hearn, J. The Gender of Oppression: Men, Masculinity, and the Critique of Marxism. New York: St. Martin's Press, 1987.

hooks, bell. "Men in Feminist Struggle—The Necessary Movement." In K. L. Hagan (ed.), Women Respond to the Men's Movement: A Feminist Collection. San Francisco: Harper San Francisco, 1992.

Jennings, P. "Men, Sex, and Rape: An ABC News Forum with Peter Jennings." May 5, 1992. Television program.

Kimmel, M., and Messner, M. "Introduction." In M. Kimmel and M. Messner (eds.), Men's Lives. New York: Macmillan, 1989.

Kupers, T. A. Revisioning Men's Lives: Gender, Intimacy and Power. New York: Guilford Press, 1993.

McLarin, K. J. "'Don't Dis Your Sis' Campaign to Fight Attacks in Public Pools." New York Times, July 14, 1993, p. B3.

May, R. J. "The Developmental Journey of the Male College Student." In R. J. May and M. Scher (eds.), Changing Roles for Men on Campus. San Francisco: Jossey-Bass, 1988.

Paglia, C. Sex, Art, and American Culture: Essays. New York: Vintage Books, 1992.

Pelka, F. "Robert Bly and Iron John." On the Issues, Summer 1991, pp. 17–19, 39.

Roiphe, K. "Date Rape's Other Victim." New York Times Sunday Magazine, June 13, 1993a, pp. 27–29, 40, 68.

Roiphe, K. The Morning After: Sex, Fear, and Feminism on Campus. Boston: Little, Brown, 1993b.

Rotundo, E. A. American Manhood: Transformations in Masculinity from the Revolution to the Modern Era. New York: Basic Books, 1993.

Ryan, W. Blaming the Victim. New York: Vintage Books, 1976.

Sanday, P. R. Fraternity Gang Rape: Sex, Brotherhood, and Privilege on Campus. New York: New York University Press, 1990.

Schur, E. M. Labeling Women Deviant: Gender, Stigma, and Social Control. New York: Random House, 1984.

Scott, J. W. Gender and the Politics of History. New York: Columbia University Press, 1988.

Seidler, V. J. Rediscovering Masculinity: Reason, Language, and Sexuality. London: Routledge, 1989.

Seidler, V. J. "Men, Feminism, and Power." In J. Hearn and D. Morgan (eds.), Men, Masculinities and Social Theory. London: Unwin Hyman, 1990.

Silverman, K. Male Subjectivity at the Margins. New York: Routledge, 1992.

Smolowe, J. "Sex with a Scorecard." Time, Apr. 5, 1993, p. 41.

Stoltenberg, J. Refusing to be a Man: Essays on Sex and Justice. Portland, Oreg.: Breitenbush Books, 1989.

Thompson, K. "What Men Really Want: A New Age Interview with Robert Bly." New Age, May 1982, pp. 30–37, 50.

Warshaw, R. I Never Called It Rape: The Ms. Report on Recognizing, Fighting and Surviving Date and Acquaintance Rape. New York: HarperCollins, 1988.

White, J. W., and Sorensen, S. B. "A Sociocultural View of Sexual Assault: From Discrepancy to Diversity." Journal of Social Issues, 1992, 48 (1), 187–195.

ROCCO L. CAPRARO is assistant dean of the college and assistant professor of history at Hobart and William Smith Colleges, where he was the founding director of the Hobart College Men and Masculinity Program.

*The underlying philosophy, content and evaluation issues, and
selection and training of facilitators for a model acquaintance rape
prevention program for men conducted at Hobart College are
described.*

A Model Acquaintance Rape Prevention Program for Men

Alan D. Berkowitz

Sexual assault and rape prevention/education programs have become com-
monplace on university and college campuses. Historically, such programs
have focused on risk reduction training for women, but there is a growing
recognition that men need to be brought into the process as well if rape is to
be prevented. Most campuses involve men through providing coed workshops.
However, a strong case can be made that single-sex groups are the most effective format for men.

Although there are few empirical evaluations of single-sex programs and
some studies have produced contradictory results, the existing literature seems
to favor the single-sex format for men. (The majority of studies evaluate coeducational programs through pre- and post-workshop assessments of rape-
related attitudes and adherence to rape myths.) Two studies suggest that men
benefit from coed programs while women show little change (Harrison,
Downes, and Williams, 1991; Holcomb, Sarvela, Sondag, and Holcomb,
1993), while others report benefits to women with no change in men's attitudes (Borden, Karr, and Caldwell-Colbert, 1988; Lenihan and others, 1992).
Lenihan and others (1992) accounted for the lack of change among men by
noting that coed workshops may increase men's defensiveness.

In two other studies, men who attended a rape prevention workshop did
not differ in their attitudes from men who had never been exposed to a program (Earle, 1992; Schaeffer and Nelson, 1993). Finally, in the only study
comparing the impact of mixed- and single-sex formats, an all-male, interactive program with peer facilitators was found to produce the only reduction in
adherence to rape-related attitudes and myths among men (this is the program

I discuss later). Thus, the cumulative research results, although tentative, suggest that all-male workshops are more likely than coed workshops to produce consistently positive effects on men. In the remainder of this chapter, I provide an overview of a model rape prevention program for men that is conducted at Hobart College and that employs all-male groups, peer facilitators, and an interactive, discussion-oriented format.

Program Description and Facilitation

How can we help college men to take responsibility for preventing rape and sexual assault on campus? A program with this goal should attempt to educate men about rape and rape myths, define the conditions that must be present for consent to sexual intimacy, increase men's empathy for sexual assault and rape victims, and encourage men to confront inappropriate, rape-supportive behaviors among peers. As the research and theory reviewed in Chapters One and Two and earlier in this chapter indicated, the program should take place in single-sex groupings, focus on men's experience, and use peer facilitators.

Thus, the model rape prevention workshop for men that I will describe is conducted in all-male groups by trained peer facilitators. It begins with a warm-up exercise that encourages the sharing of thoughts and feelings about rape prevention. This exercise is followed by factual information and discussion of a video that portrays a campus rape. Workshop facilitators attempt to establish an atmosphere of openness and nondefensiveness that will encourage all men to speak and participate, and men's responsibility for preventing rape is emphasized throughout the workshop in a variety of ways. Discussion of the video focuses on defining consent, understanding the victim's experience, and examining the ways in which men pressure each other to be sexually active. Male college staff and faculty participate in the program as mentors and facilitator trainers, and a staff member attends each workshop but does not ordinarily participate.

In achieving the desired participation and discussion, all-male workshops have a number of advantages. They allow men to speak openly without fear of judgment or criticism by women, make it less likely that men will be passive or quiet, and avoid the gender-based polarization that may reinforce men's rape-prone attitudes. In addition, a diversity of opinions and viewpoints can be expressed, reflecting men's variety of attitudes and beliefs about appropriate sexual relationships and allowing participants to deconstruct the monolithic image of masculinity the media have presented to them. Programs that use respected student leaders as role models can also influence participants by the way these leaders model appropriate attitudes and behaviors and suggest alternative ways of being male.

There is evidence that many men are uncomfortable with other men's bragging about sexual exploits, dislike men's preoccupation with commenting on women's bodies, and misperceive the extent of other men's sexual activity

(Berkowitz, in press; also see Chapter Six). In addition, most men are probably not likely to rape or sexually assault (see Chapter One). These men may belong to a silent majority, who keep their discomfort to themselves rather than express disagreement or intervene in an environment that they perceive as unsympathetic. An important outcome of effective rape prevention work is to increase the numbers of men with positive attitudes who decide to step out of this closet of silence.

The Hobart College program that I present here as a model was begun in 1983 as a voluntary workshop and is now required of all first-year men. A separate program facilitated by a team of women students and staff is required for all first-year women. Hobart (a men's college) and William Smith (a women's college) are coordinate liberal arts colleges that share a common campus, faculty and curriculum, and student services, but have separate deans' offices, housing, student governments, admissions offices, and athletic programs. The coordinate structure of Hobart and William Smith Colleges provides an opportunity to examine the different needs and experiences of men and women and influenced the development of separate programs for each gender. The underlying philosophy that guides the men's rape prevention program was presented in Chapter Two.

The workshop is presented by a number of different facilitators to small groups of men (primarily in residence halls) and prior to an individual workshop, its facilitators may meet with a resident adviser, fraternity officers, or other sponsors for that individual workshop to discuss potential problems and issues or review program content. Ideally, these sponsors will have already attended a workshop themselves and be familiar with program goals and procedures. Sponsors are also present during the workshop itself and are invited to debriefings. The following outline offers an overview of the workshop (a detailed workshop outline, given to facilitators, appears in the Appendix to this volume).

    I. Warm-up. "What's difficult about being a first-year male on this campus?"
    II. Introduction of facilitators and overview of workshop
    III. Definitions of rape, sexual assault, sexual harassment, and statistics about their incidence in college
    IV. Introduction of video
    V. Discussion of video
    VI. Definition of consent
    VII. Optional rerun of video
    VIII. Summary of relevant college policies
    IX. Summary, wrap-up, and evaluation

The workshop begins with a brief introduction followed by a warm-up exercise that gives participants the opportunity to share their feelings about being a man on campus (alternate warm-up exercises are provided in the outline in the Appendix). Often first-year men express frustration with women or with heterosexual dating situations, and fears of being falsely accused of rape. The warm-up reduces these men's sense of isolation by underscoring their common concerns, and it promotes a norm of men listening to each other. During the warm-up, it is important for facilitators to gently direct the group when inappropriate comments or interruptions are made. At the end of the warm-up, facilitators summarize the common themes and concerns expressed.

Next, facilitators introduce themselves in more detail, review the workshop outline, provide definitions of acquaintance rape and sexual assault, and review studies of the incidence of rape on campus. The video is then introduced and shown. Selection of an appropriate video is an extremely important task. Chapter Seven reviews a number of videos that can be appropriate for all-male programs. *Aftereffects*, the video used in Hobart's program, contains a number of typical male–male interactions about sexual conquests, shows the victim's trauma after the rape, and has scenarios in which other men confront the perpetrator. It thus provides excellent opportunities to discuss many of the sociocultural issues affecting men's proclivity to rape. This discussion is the most important part of the workshop. Initially, participants are asked if they think the portrayal was plausible and realistic. Criticisms are often made of the filming and staging, but facilitators should not dwell upon these comments. Important discussion items include how the victim's choice of clothing is perceived, the role of alcohol, common rape myths (such as the meaning of no), differences in motivation between the perpetrator and victim, the continuum of sexually assaultive behaviors, and whether what happened constitutes rape. Facilitators often suggest modifications to the video scenes to create more ambiguity and provoke controversy if the group reaches consensus about what happened and there is a resulting lack of discussion. It is left up to the judgment of the facilitators to decide when to introduce specific topics and points.

One of the most important components of the workshop is the presentation of guidelines for consent. Focusing on a consent model for sexual behavior allows the workshop to avoid legalistic discussions about what constitutes coercion and encourages students to define desired behavior positively. Consent is present when both parties are fully conscious, both parties are equally free to act (the woman is not coerced or constrained), and both parties have positively and clearly communicated their intent. The model is presented as an ideal which, when approximated, reduces the likelihood that a man will be accused of sexual assault. Discussion can be extremely heated, and many students object to the implication that substance use makes consent impossible. However, the model helps men understand that rape is more than miscommunication and that abuse of power is involved. The discussion of the video concludes with a focus on how men can respond to sexual peer pressure. Men often do not realize how the behavior of a minority of men can cause women to stereotype the majority, and learning this point encourages men to realize that they themselves are indirect victims of perpetrators.

After discussion of the full video, facilitators have the option of showing an abbreviated version that highlights certain events for a second time, but usually, there is so much discussion that this is not necessary. The workshop concludes with a review of campus resources, an invitation to participants who wish to consider becoming facilitators, and an evaluation questionnaire.

Program Evaluation

As I noted earlier, this program was evaluated in a recent study by Earle (1992) that compared three different program formats with a nontreatment (control) group. The Hobart program was single-sex and used small groups, interactive techniques, and trained male peers as facilitators. The second program also employed group discussion and interaction in similar-sized groups, but was coed and employed student services professionals as facilitators. The third program was coed and employed large groups and a lecture format with student services professionals as facilitators. The pre- and post-workshop measure assessed attitudes toward rape and toward women and incorporated questions from the Attitudes Towards Rape Scale (ATR) and the Attitudes Towards Women Scale (AWS-S). The ATR scale (Barnett and Field, 1977) assesses agreement or disagreement with a variety of statements that reflect societal attitudes toward rape. The AWS-S scale assesses attitudes towards women in a number of spheres, including their vocational, educational, and intellectual roles, their freedom and independence, and issues of dating, courtship, and etiquette. Earle's study used the simplified version of the AWS-S scale developed by Nelson (1988). Both scales have been tested extensively for reliability and validity.

Each treatment was administered at a different college. A total of 694 male participants completed both the pre- and posttests. The pretest was conducted in the first week of October 1991, two weeks before the workshop, and administered by resident advisers at floor meetings. The posttest was administered immediately following the workshop or in a subsequent floor meeting for the control group. Factor analysis identified three factors that could be used to assess change between the pre- and posttests: the first factor assessed the traditional home and work roles of women (accounting for 33 percent of the variance), the second assessed motives for rape (accounting for 17 percent of the variance), and the third assessed the perceived severity of the crime of rape (also accounting for 17 percent of the variance). The data analysis employed multiple analysis of variance (MANOVA). There were no significant differences in pretest scores between students at the four schools studied. On the posttest, only the men in the Hobart program exhibited a significant liberalization of attitudes when compared with the control group. These men had changed in a positive direction on the factor assessing traditional home and work roles of women and on the factor assessing motives for rape. Interestingly, the factor corresponding to perceptions of the severity of rape as a crime did not improve for any college, and became significantly less liberal among the men in the coed, large-group lecture format.

This study strongly points to the effectiveness of all-male rape prevention programs and supports previous research in suggesting that coed formats may not be effective in changing men's attitudes.

Facilitator Selection and Training

In the Hobart program, facilitators are recruited from groups of student leaders and from workshop audiences. Initially, the program began with a small group of facilitators (three to five) and was offered to residence halls and fraternities to satisfy institutional requirements for educational programs. As more men experienced the workshop, additional facilitators were recruited, and the workshop was eventually required for all first-year men. Currently, there are fifteen to thirty student facilitators each year who are divided into groups of three to four, with each group supervised by a staff member or professor. Each year, a core of five to ten experienced facilitators provides continuity for the program and helps train new members.

Although no formal application and screening process exists, careful attention is paid to the attitudes, reputations, and past experiences of men who want to facilitate the workshop. Occasionally men seek involvement inappropriately, as a way of working out their own issues as a perpetrator or a friend of a victim or as a way of gaining status on campus. While such motivations are not automatically problematic, they need to be explored carefully.

Training takes place at a series of four to six dinner meetings, which are followed by practice sessions. The first dinner meeting emphasizes trust building and consciousness raising and focuses on men's reasons for getting involved in the rape prevention workshop. Subsequent meetings feature presentations on men's issues and experiences, a review of the literature on rape proclivity among college men (including rape myths, personality characteristics, situational variables, and related concepts), and an overview of rape trauma syndrome. This formal large-group training concludes with a session on group facilitation and discussion skills that includes an opportunity for more experienced facilitators to share their insights and techniques. (These effective facilitation techniques are reviewed at greater length in Chapter Four).

Following the formal training period, facilitators are assigned to their small groups of three or four, which meet to divide up responsibility for different sections of the workshop and to practice together. A supervising faculty or staff member is available for consultation. Prior to the first scheduled workshops, a dress rehearsal is held, with experienced facilitators presenting the workshop in its entirety to the group.

The Hobart College rape prevention workshop is offered to all first-year men over a period of three to five evenings, with each small group of facilitators presenting simultaneously in residence hall lounges to groups of fifteen to twenty men. Following each presentation, facilitators meet with their faculty or staff mentor (who is present as an observer during the workshop) to discuss process issues, handling of difficult questions, and other problems. All the facilitators meet together the following evening, prior to that evening's set of workshops, to discuss how things are going and to explore common issues and concerns. This process continues until all the workshops have been completed.

The training process emphasizes facilitation and group-discussion skills over content. Facilitators grow in confidence and experience as workshops are presented, discussed, and reviewed. Staff and faculty mentors participate in the training process throughout and must be willing to examine and share their own attitudes and experiences around issues of masculinity and rape. On those rare occasions when workshops get too heated or prove difficult for facilitators in other ways, the observing mentor can step in to provide structure and guidance.

Conclusion

The guidelines provided in this chapter can help colleges and universities implement a model rape prevention program for men that uses small-group discussion formats and trained peer facilitators. An empirical study conducted to evaluate the effectiveness of the model program supports other research and theory that suggests that all-male, peer-facilitated programs are the intervention of choice for college men.

The impact of a one-time educational workshop, however, is limited by definition. Possible follow-ups could include a coed discussion or skills training to help men confront male peer pressure and rape-supportive beliefs. Most men who evaluate the Hobart program express satisfaction with the all-male format but indicate a desire to discuss the issue further with women. A second limitation is that the workshop explicitly addresses only heterosexual date rape. Facilitators do mention in the course of the workshop that rape can also take place in same-sex pairs, and facilitators are trained to avoid the heterosexism that can occur when people make implicit assumptions about heterosexuality. Finally, while educational programs and workshops may ameliorate the rape-prone attitudes and beliefs of most men, other men, with more entrenched personality characteristics associated with rape proclivity (see Chapter One), are not likely to be affected. These men need intensive treatment that utilizes clinical models such as the one presented in Chapter Five.

References

Barnett, N. J., and Field, H. S. "Sex Differences in University Students' Attitudes Towards Rape." Journal of College Student Personnel, 1977, 18, 93–96.

Berkowitz, A. D. "The Role of Coaches in Rape Prevention Programs for Athletes." In A. Parrot, N. Cummings, and T. Marchell (eds.), *Rape 101: Sexual Assault Prevention for College Athletes.* Holmes Beach, Fla.: Learning Publications, in press.

Borden, L. A., Karr, S. K., and Caldwell-Colbert, A. T. "Effects of a University Rape Prevention Program on Attitudes and Empathy Toward Rape." *Journal of College Student Development,* 1988, *29,* 132–138.

Earle, J. P. "Acquaintance Rape Workshops: Their Effectiveness in Changing the Attitudes of First Year College Men." Thesis submitted to the University of Connecticut, 1992.

Harrison, P. J., Downes, J. D., and Williams, M. D. "Date and Acquaintance Rape: Perceptions and Attitude Change Strategies." *Journal of College Student Development,* 1991, *32,* 131–139.

Holcomb, D. R., Sarvela. P. D., Sondag, A., and Holcomb, L.C.H. "An Evaluation of a Mixed-Gender Date Rape Prevention Workshop." *Journal of American College Health,* 1993, *41,* 159–164.

Lenihan, G. O., Rawlins, M. E., Eberly, C. G., Buckley, B., and Masters, B. "Gender Differences in Rape Supportive Attitudes Before and After a Date Rape Education Intervention." *Journal of College Student Development.* 1992, *33,* 331–338.

Nelson, M. C. "Reliability and Validity and Cross-Cultural Comparisons for the Simplified Attitudes Towards Women Scale." *Sex Roles,* 1988, *18,* 289–296.

Schaeffer, A. M., and Nelson, E. S. "Rape-Supportive Attitudes: Effects of On-campus Residence and Education." *Journal of College Student Development,* 1993, *34,* 175–179.

ALAN D. BERKOWITZ is counseling center director and assistant professor of psychology at Hobart and William Smith Colleges.

The experiences of three student facilitators for Hobart College's Rape Prevention Program offer additional insights into the workshop's methodology and effect on participants.

Student Perspectives on Facilitating Rape Prevention Programs

Adam K. Simon, Jack Paris, Charles A. Ramsay

Student facilitators have a special perspective on acquaintance rape prevention programs for college men because they understand the feelings and experiences of their fellow students even though they themselves have made the transition from not understanding that rape is men's problem to having that understanding. In this chapter, three men with extensive experience in facilitating Hobart College's rape prevention workshop discuss how they came to be facilitators and describe the most important and most difficult aspects of these workshops and the techniques they have used to make the workshops effective for their peers.

Adam K. Simon's Perspective

Six years ago, my girlfriend was raped. She knew her assailant and felt the rape was her fault. It was difficult for us to talk about the incident; therefore, we usually did not. She was my friend, but I could not, or did not know how to, help her. My involvement with the Hobart College rape prevention program began when three fraternity members presented the mandatory workshop in my residence hall during my freshman year at Hobart. I remember thinking that if fraternity guys, who I thought were too macho to be concerned about women's experience, could talk about rape then so could I. During that workshop discussion, I realized that my efforts to help my friend three years earlier had made matters worse for her. I learned that by threatening to hurt her attacker I was not helping her and that, unintentionally, I was forcing her to remember the incident and continue to relive the agony of the moment. In addition, my questions about what she was wearing placed so much guilt on her that she could not turn to me for help. After the presentation, I knew that I wanted to help other men to prevent rape as well as help their friends deal with rape.

Traditionally, rape has been viewed as a women's problem. The environment at Hobart College is unique in that men are encouraged to take responsibility for rape prevention. The gender studies curriculum forces men to challenge societal norms that make women second-class citizens. Furthermore, social events encourage discussion about classroom topics in forums such as the acquaintance rape workshops. My interest in learning about rape came from my own guilt about hurting someone I had wanted to help. However, without the atmosphere of acceptance that Hobart and William Smith Colleges provide I would not have found a way to act on my concerns.

When I became a facilitator, I learned that the key to facilitation is getting the group interested and involved. To begin a discussion, an icebreaker is generally the first order of business. In the rape prevention workshop, asking each member of the group to comment on what is difficult about being a first-year man is a good way to start. The question always draws similar responses that focus on the men's difficulties in meeting women. Throughout this exercise, and the entire meeting, it is important for facilitators to show enthusiasm and insight about students' responses. For example, making eye contact with each respondent and giving feedback such as, "I remember feeling the same way," or, "It sounds as though you feel the same as other members of the group," are excellent ways to involve people in the topic. When discussing acquaintance rape, it is important for facilitators to remember that there will be rapists in the room. Rather than single out individuals for past negative behavior, I have found it best to talk about "men in general." The statistics that are provided highlight the prevalence of rape and sexual assault, and the discussion is then used to work on prevention strategies.

After four years of involvement in the Hobart program, I have found that no man will initially accept the idea that he rapes women. Statistics, personal accounts, and research that show that acquaintance rapes occur are all blocked out. Therefore, it is the facilitator's job to make a connection, even a simplistic one, between the individual and the act of rape. This usually comes through men's being helped to understand how words form attitudes and how men's language can encourage rape. The example I use is that not everyone is as strong-willed and intelligent as the person to whom I may be speaking. A man may know the difference between saying, "I'd like to get on her," and knowing it is not acceptable to force himself on another person. However, when he verbally puts women down, he may encourage other men to believe that is the way men are supposed to think. They may come to believe this is the way women want to be treated and think, Other men put women down, why shouldn't I? Showing the influence that men have over other men is one way facilitators create understanding about the difficult topic of rape.

Acquaintance rape occurs because one group uses power in a negative way over another. A good facilitator often uses his influence and standing as a student leader in a positive way to promote a change in the way men use power. The workshops occur during the fall of the first year when students are very impressionable. The most effective facilitators are those whom students look up to. Athletes and fraternity members, for example, are social heroes to many first-year students. It is extremely convincing for first-year men to hear their social heroes, men who are not usually outspoken about curbing violence say that acquaintance rape is something men should be discussing, more convincing than it is to hear staff or women students talk on the same issue.

Finally, being a good facilitator means being enthused and concerned about the topic. Asking the group to respond to an individual's question is an excellent technique to spark other people's enthusiasm. Also, it is important to remember that each student enters the discussion at a different level of understanding about the topic and to keep these differences in mind when setting goals. If a facilitator's goal is to raise men's consciousness of, and interest in, acquaintance rape, he will never be disappointed.

Jack Paris's Perspective

Participation in the Hobart rape prevention program has taught me many things about myself as well as about other men. First, it has shown me the powerful presence and solidity of traditional male notions concerning women's rights and privileges. Second, through watching the workshops in action, I have seen that it is actually possible to alter men's stereotypes about women and to begin the process of cognitive and behavioral change in men. Men are not brutal animals or Cro-Magnon primitives, as many seem to think, but are in fact capable of changing when shown the error of media and societal norms concerning women. The key issue for me is to educate as many people as possible and then let the changes happen. If it can work for me, then I am pretty sure that it can also work for other members of our society and college community.

Once one truly learns about acquaintance rape, people's rights are seen in a different way. I have certainly seen changes in my own perceptions of women at school and at home and in the way I view society at large since I began to learn about rape through this program. I'm as conservative and traditional as anyone, but through my exploration of the phenomena of acquaintance rape, my views about women and society have improved. If I can change myself, I believe everybody else can as well. If a man realizes he is in the wrong about a particular issue, then he should also realize that the sensible thing is for him to alter his views. I hope this is what happens as more men learn about acquaintance rape.

I worked as a program facilitator at Hobart in 1988 and 1989, and I felt that the program was important for college campuses and important for my school. The subject of acquaintance rape is not easy to talk about, but it seemed to be an issue that could be communicated to other students and be addressed with a persuasive program. The common theme that I took away from my participation was that there needs to be much more education on this topic, and that many men have never really looked at the issue, even when they have been involved in an acquaintance rape.

Any time a large group of college-age men speak about any subject involving sex (even tangentially), it is important that a serious tone be set from the beginning or the audience will never take the program seriously. I never really appreciated being told what to do in college—specifically because it was my first experience with total freedom—and for anyone to discuss how I should behave while dating was almost taboo to me. In a first-year college dorm, most people do not want to be told how to behave. Thus, for the workshop to be effective, the initial moments are critical.

Obviously, it is extremely difficult to communicate the idea that acquaintance rape has nothing to do with sex per se and that it is a recognized crime. Most men do not believe this, so when I facilitated, I used examples to illustrate the point. Success with a college audience requires that the facilitator get the workshop participants to the point where they can separate the sexual encounter from the actions taken by the couple during the time preceding that encounter. I also tried to get across the point that, no matter what a man does for a woman on a date, he is not entitled to sex. As I mentioned above, it is very difficult to make these points to men who are mostly experiencing freedom for the first time and are in a setting where social interaction is a critical aspect of their lives. College men, I feel, will always be hesitant, or even hostile, when initially presented with the topic of acquaintance rape.

After trying to make the point that dating and spending money and time on a woman do not give a man the right to sex, I worked to hold the audience's attention as much as possible. Some of the more provocative statistics and facts worked well for this. I also liked to stress the fact that acquaintance rape is criminal and that the consequences can be severe and alter the rest of a person's life. Further, since the topic is so sensitive (for all, including the facilitator), I found that keeping a good tone and pace was critical or else the audience would turn off.

Another reason acquaintance rape will always be difficult to discuss is that the notion of sex always underlies the discussion. College men may be the most difficult audience to communicate to concerning this crime even though they are the group that needs to listen to the realities of acquaintance rape the most. In the workshops, there always seemed to be a great tension between the subject and the target group, which made the facilitator's job extremely challenging. I always tried to keep in mind that the program really could make a difference, was worthwhile for everybody at the school and, at the same time, rewarding for me. I developed enough interest in acquaintance rape to write a college research paper and to participate in a panel on the subject. Following my graduation in 1989, I worked at a rape crisis center as a hot-line volunteer, following a fairly extensive training period. After I finished my first year of law school, I worked as a certified intern in a district attorney's office, assisting in the prosecution of various sex crimes including acquaintance rape. I felt that the Hobart and William Smith program was an excellent foundation for my future activities and that it has had a positive effect on all those who facilitated or participated in it.

Charles A. Ramsay's Perspective

There are many reasons why I became a facilitator. During my first year at Hobart College, a good friend of mine was dismissed from school, charged with raping a woman on a date. He was a baseball player and an all-around popular guy, and most of the men I knew blamed the woman because "she had made the first move." I might have felt the same way except for the fact that I was friends with her as well and knew that she would not tell such a story unless it were true. I witnessed two people who were close to me go through a tremendous amount of pain simply because one person failed to understand what no really meant.

In my sophomore year, I was a resident adviser. Sitting in while my first-year residents participated in the acquaintance rape prevention workshop, I was shocked at how many of the first-year men stated that rape never happens on our campus. I was also a fraternity member who suddenly realized that many of the things that men say and do when they are alone with one another contribute to the rape culture that is present on every campus in the country. Once, in a span of only ten minutes in a conversation among men, I counted seventeen words or phrases describing women as sexual objects. There are many other reasons why I got involved in the Hobart rape prevention program as a student and why I continue to remain involved in it as a college administrator. Each time I facilitate a discussion, I learn more about the subject of rape and how it affects different people. No workshop has ever been exactly the same. Sometimes, I finish a workshop feeling as if I have had a dramatic impact on the men who participated and, at other times, I feel as if I have accomplished nothing. The point is that, no matter how slight it may be, I feel I am making a difference. It is healthy to realize that one cannot change the world with a single workshop. Nevertheless, if one man thinks twice about having unwanted sex with a woman, then something has been accomplished. It means that person is more aware of the problem of acquaintance rape than he was before. To me, it is tremendously rewarding to know that I may have prevented a rape.

I had many fears before giving my first workshop, the greatest of which was the fear that I would be completely ineffective and that no one would take what I had to say seriously. As I pointed out earlier, most men on college campuses do not believe that rape is a serious problem at their schools. When they think of a rapist, they think of a psychopath who jumps out from behind bushes to attack women. A good friend of mine once told me that she wishes she could tell which men are rapists and which are not—the point being that there is not a particular type of male who rapes. That is what makes the topic of acquaintance rape so disturbing to men—the fact that a friend, some guy they know or trust, can commit a rape and probably not even know it. That is why this program is so essential on college campuses.

Another fear that I had when first presenting was simply that I lacked facilitation skills and would not be able to articulate my thoughts clearly to the audience. It is always nerve-racking to stand up in front of a group of people and talk, especially when you must talk about a volatile and personal issue such as rape. One thing that helped me was knowing that I was not alone up there in front of the room. I had two other facilitators working with me and between the three of us, with the administrative advisor in the back, we had plenty to say. Once we got a workshop rolling, everything seemed to fall into place. I also found it important to remember that I was there as a facilitator, not a speaker. The most successful programs that I have facilitated were the ones where the audience did about 90 percent of the talking. The facilitator's job is to present the data and the topics of discussion and then get the group talking. I was never afraid to call on someone and ask him a question. Even if someone said something completely absurd, I would bounce it around the room and ask other members of the audience what they thought. Once I had a man say, "If I ask a woman if she wants sex, and she says no, I take her to my room and nail her anyway." I was angry, but rather than argue with him myself, I asked others what they thought about what he had just said. Almost everyone in the room spoke out against him.

A good way to get the program started and to ease tensions is to ask a question and go around the room until everyone has answered it. We usually ask, "What's difficult about being a first-year male on campus?" or, "Do you think rape is a problem on this campus?" This icebreaker gets everyone talking and is often a good way to get a sense of the audience and figure out how to get the discussion rolling afterwards. After the icebreaker and the introduction, the video on acquaintance rape is shown, and it is much easier to get people talking after the viewing, referring back to the video and asking questions to facilitate discussion. Facilitators who are running out of questions and have a group that does not seem to want to talk should not be afraid to twist the video's situations and present different scenarios that might stir up controversy among the group. For example, a facilitator could ask, "What if the woman had been drinking large quantities of alcohol, and she didn't say no to the man? Would it be rape then?"

Another effective way to get people talking is to throw in facts and figures about rape. For example, one out of every three women will be sexually assaulted. Facts like that often surprise men and get them talking about the issue. I also like to read the definitions of rape and consent. Sometimes it is best to read these definitions in the beginning, but I occasionally like to see what some of the men's own definitions are before reading the workshop's definitions, so sometimes I will read them towards the end.

Probably the most controversial subject in the workshops is the role of alcohol in consent and rape. Since Hobart and William Smith Colleges are located in New York State, I often give the New York State law that says that if a woman is legally drunk then she is incapable of giving consent. This means that if a man has sex with a woman while she is drunk he could be committing rape. This law is guaranteed to get some people talking because it scares men no end to think that if they pick up a woman at a party and she has been drinking they can be accused of rape. Most workshop participants will undoubtedly say that this law is unfair to men. I have spent literally entire workshops talking about this single issue, which is fine, because I believe that it strikes at the heart of the problem. Alcohol is involved in 90 percent of the acquaintance rapes that occur on college campuses and often plays a role in the miscommunication that happens when an acquaintance rape is committed.

This perspective from which this law is written is usually very difficult to justify in the eyes of the first-year college men. I suggest that, if they want to discuss what is and is not fair, they should consider how unfair our society is to women in general. I ask how many of them are afraid to walk around campus at night. How many of them go to their cars at night with a key clenched between their fingers ready to lash out at an attacker? Men do not think about how privileged they are to be able to live without the fear of assault. They should not feel threatened by the law because, in most cases, a woman will not accuse the man of rape either because she believes it was a mistake she made or because she blames herself for what happened. To come forth and accuse a man of rape is extremely traumatizing. The woman often will have to recreate the rape in her mind and in front of others, which can be terrifying. Most people in our culture blame the woman for the rape, saying that she "turned him on" or that she was "asking for it" because she was drunk or wearing "promiscuous" clothing. In fact, the law has traditionally favored the man. If one looks at the law in this light, it suddenly does not seem so heavily weighted in favor of the woman. Even if the men in the audience do not like the law, they will at least think about it. Perhaps next time they are with a woman who is intoxicated, they will think twice before having sex.

Maybe the most important questions to ask in the workshop are, "Why do you want to have sex in the first place? Is it to satisfy your ego? Is it because your friends have put pressure on you to do so? Or is it because you really like the woman and are attracted to her? If you do like her, wouldn't it be more satisfying and meaningful to both of you to have sex when you are sober?" These are questions that can be asked any time during the workshop, but they are sometimes particularly effective as a close. When closing, I find that it is also important to solicit questions or comments to share with the group. It is also critical to mention counseling and support services available on campus to help people cope with a rape. Some men in the room may have friends who have been raped, and it is always possible (indeed, likely) that a member of the audience has committed an acquaintance rape and, because of the program, has only now realized what he has done. Therefore, it is critical that facilitators give participants the names of services or people that they can speak with.

Sometimes, I feel that I need another hour to talk; other times, I feel that the workshop cannot end soon enough. I have left workshops feeling exhilarated, and I have left them feeling drained and worn-out, but I always feel good about doing a workshop, even if initially I feel that little was accomplished. Again, I know I cannot change the world with one workshop. Change takes a long time, particularly when the problem is so pervasive. Nevertheless, after every workshop, I feel that I have learned something new. I am not an expert on rape nor are the other facilitators. Sometimes, I believe that I get more out of the workshops than the audiences, which is one reason why I continue to do them. The other reason is that I know acquaintance rape can be prevented. Men simply need to stop assuming that they know what women are thinking and, instead, come right out and ask them what they are thinking. Rape is a men's issue, and men can stop rape if they take the time to communicate with each other and with women. The acquaintance rape prevention workshop teaches men that they need to, and can, stop rape from happening.

ADAM K. SIMON graduated from Hobart College in 1993 and currently works in the computer industry. As a student, he served as a leader in his fraternity and was elected to the position of student trustee.

JACK PARIS is a lawyer and a 1989 Hobart College graduate. His perspective combines his thoughts from his senior year and more recent reflections.

CHARLES A. RAMSAY, a 1992 Hobart College graduate, is assistant director of admissions for Hobart and William Smith Colleges and is still active in the acquaintance rape prevention workshop.

A treatment protocol for rape and other violence perpetrators is proposed. Philosophy, assessment, and a treatment curriculum are examined along with resistance to such treatment programs.

Treatment for Perpetrators of Rape and Other Violence

Jeffrey W. Pollard

Interpersonal violence, particularly rape and battering, is one of the most difficult behaviors for college and university officials to address. Traditionally, counselors have viewed treatment related to these behaviors as a service that should be voluntary rather than mandated and as more appropriate for victims and survivors than for perpetrators. This perspective both reflects and contributes to an institutional system that is unwilling to look at the causes of violence and then intervene strategically. To rectify the problem, the American College Personnel Association's Campus Violence Project has encouraged campuses to establish formal violence prevention programs (Pollard, 1991; Roark, 1991).

In this chapter, I explore the challenges associated with providing campus-based treatment for those who commit acts of violence. Topics discussed include institutional resistance to treatment of violent students; philosophies of violence and how they apply to perpetrator treatment; perpetrator assessment, including issues of lethality and substance abuse; and campus-specific considerations for perpetrator treatment. In addition, I suggest a treatment curriculum, including specific elements intended to help administrators assess the feasibility of providing a treatment program.

Institutional Impediments to Effective Perpetrator Treatment

University and college administrators and faculty who become aware of violent students have the responsibility to ensure that treatment is provided for these students, in order to protect others from further victimization as well as to aid the perpetrator in gaining a perspective into himself and his responsibilities to society. In fact, campuses that expel known offenders without attempting to ensure that they receive appropriate treatment may be guilty of simply passing the problem on to others, adding to society's pool of identified but untreated violent individuals. This is equivalent to what would happen if a state identified, tried, and convicted a perpetrator of domestic violence and then only banished him from that state, leaving the remaining forty-nine states to deal with the problem. Perpetrators should not be treated as though they were toxic waste, to be removed from our site only to be dumped on our neighboring institutions (Pollard and Whitaker, in press). When untreated perpetrators are simply expelled, they can enroll in another school instantly, where they will almost certainly victimize someone again, because when a person is interpersonally violent, the likelihood that he will repeat his crimes escalates in both frequency and magnitude (Walker, 1979).

No institution of higher education wants another institution's perpetrator, but in today's atmosphere of shrinking enrollment and pressure on admissions departments to bring in the class, such individuals can slip past the best admissions officer. To rectify this, universities and colleges can make it clear to each other that identified perpetrators who have not completed treatment for their violence are not eligible for enrollment on another campus. Indeed, higher education has a unique opportunity to begin the difficult task of bringing an end to the cycle of violence. However, institutional reluctance to provide treatment may reflect a larger societal ambivalence about addressing issues of violence. As Lore and Schultz (1993) have noted, "most Americans, including those at all levels of education and government as well as most social scientists, seem convinced that aggression either cannot or should not be controlled. As a result, they fail even to consider a variety of potentially effective measures that could reduce violence in the United States" (p. 16.).

Epidemiology of Interpersonal Violence. Empirical estimates of violence between partners vary greatly (Hershberger, 1988; Marshall, 1988). Deschner (1984) estimated that between 2 and 4 percent of all couples experience violence. When Straus and his associates studied partner and marital violence, they estimated that between 11 and 12 percent of wives reported incidents of violence during the previous year and 28 percent over the course of their marriages (Straus and Gelles, 1986; Straus, Gelles, and Steinmetz, 1980). Walker (1979) reported that over half of all women are physically abused by their partners at some time in their lives. A survey of college students in 1985 (Bogel-Allbritten and Allbritten, 1986) found that 61 percent had personal knowledge of at least one other student involved in a violent relationship. Women who as children witnessed abuse within their families are at higher risk than other women of distrusting men and marriage or being victims within dating and marital relationships (Jaffe, Wolfe, and Wilson, 1990). Men who as children witnessed violence in their families are at increased risk of becoming violent themselves (Finkelhor, Hotaling, and Yllo, 1988; Sonkin,

Martin, and Walker, 1985). *Any* abuse is too much, and the physical and social imbalances inherent in a man raping or beating a woman make the necessity of intervention even greater.

Ethical Concerns. Some argue that it is unethical to mandate treatment for someone who is violent when it is not possible to predict perfectly that individual's potential for future violence (Gilbert, 1992). Applying this same logic to the criminal justice system would require that we abandon incarceration, based on the fact that some individuals commit a crime only once. This approach to treatment ignores the rights and needs of the victims and potential victims of violence perpetrators. Treatment should not be withheld from a rapist simply because he does not want it, inasmuch as without it he will most likely rape again. We have an obligation to his next victim, whoever she may be, to try to help him. Incarceration will prevent his raping a member of the public as long as he is in jail, but by the time he is released—and he will be— the public and, specifically, past and potential victims have the expectation, if not the right, that some innovative treatment specialist will have found a way to help him stop raping.

Provider Resistance. Some treatment providers argue that they only oppose mandatory treatment for adult, competent, not-at-risk clients (Gilbert, 1992). It is also likely, however, that many professionals do not want to deal with their resistance to treat certain individuals, that is, they do not wish to examine their thoughts and feelings regarding violence perpetrators' behavior. Some professionals even use their resistance as an argument, saying that they cannot do a good job of treating individuals they do not want to treat. Therefore, perpetrators should not be mandated for treatment because providers do not want to treat them. But who is responsible for providers' unwillingness to treat? Who should experience the consequences of this unwillingness? Victims? There may be no other group that is systematically denied treatment on such a widespread basis as those who perpetrate violence. If we are to hold individuals responsible for their behavior, then therapists, too, must be held responsible for their behavior. Clearly, some providers are simply unable to deal with these issues, but those who reject difficult cases based on political grounds, an unwillingness to deal with problematic clients, or the lack of outcome certainty should rethink their commitment to preventing victimization through perpetrator treatment. The perspective that advocates precluding mandatory treatment of undesirable clients simply ensures that there will always be victims and consequently always be clients for those who will treat only victims.

There are also those who argue that mandated treatment does not work because the coercive element prevents the creation of a therapeutic relationship. Yet, evaluations of mandated programs found pre- and posttreatment changes in measures of self-esteem, locus of control, depression, anger or hostility, jealousy, and preference for egalitarian gender roles (Williams, 1985; Saunders and Hanusa, 1986; Neidig, 1986). Several investigations have also demonstrated success in short-term, cognitive-behavioral group formats (Edelson, Miller, Stone, and Chapman, 1985; Deschner and McNeil, 1986; Williams, 1985; Saunders and Hanusa, 1986; Dutton, 1986; Hershberger, 1988).

University and college counseling centers are often reluctant to accept mandated referrals, claiming that forcing a perpetrator to enter treatment sends him the message that control works. Unfortunately, these men are experienced in the use of control. To the extent that perpetrators find being forced to participate distasteful, that experience can be useful in creating empathy in them for victims they have controlled through violence. In fact, 83 percent of counseling center directors report that they accept some form of mandatory referral in their counseling centers for substance abuse treatment, and despite some treatment providers' dissatisfaction with this trend, 62 percent of these directors report moderate success with these cases (Gallagher, 1991). Most violent individuals will enter treatment only by coercion, and the most logical provider of treatment within the college setting is the college counseling center.

Providers' current reluctance to treat violent offenders may parallel their earlier unwillingness to address issues of chemical use when graduate counseling programs did not comprehensively prepare providers to treat addiction and substance abuse. Similarly, because they lack appropriate training and have a traditional reluctance to deal with violence perpetrators, providers may simply not be aware of the treatment issues involved (Cerio, 1988). Consequently, counseling centers are often ill-equipped to work with violent students even when such a student presents voluntarily. Yet most of the necessary techniques already exist within counselors' repertoires. It is a matter of providers' ordering these techniques differently, becoming familiar with the issues, and most importantly, acquiring a willingness to help and a belief that change is possible (a belief held by most providers in most cases). Under those circumstances, providers may bring about a positive alteration in perpetrators' patterns of violence.

The following discussion suggests basic content for a campus-based treatment program. These suggestions do not represent a fully formed procedure. Because counseling centers have made few attempts to carry out such programs, empirical inquiry and refinement are still necessary before a standard of practice can be established. However, the broad guidelines that follow are a first step toward establishing a philosophy of treatment, assessment of perpetrators, and the actual treatment of perpetrators within institutions of higher education.

Philosophy of Violence Treatment

For the purposes of this chapter, violence is defined by its impact on the victim, not its etiology. It is any act that controls a victim or causes her to experience fear. It may take sexual, physical, or psychological forms and often conforms to a pattern that is coherent, understandable, and purposeful. The goal of violence is to intimidate and undermine, to keep the victim down and under control. Roark (1991) also suggests that violence be defined as "behavior which by intent, action, and/or outcome harms a person," and she comments on the "three essential elements" of the definition, each of which leads "to different forms of intervention by campus authorities: Intent to harm is best addressed through education, action which harms through judicial procedures, and outcome, through counseling and other services [that is, treatment]" (p. 3.)

Counseling Versus Education. As Roark points out, and as is described in more detail later in this chapter, treatment of a perpetrator's intent to use interpersonal violence uses education and differs from counseling and psychotherapy, thereby representing another modality of counseling center service programming. Confusion may exist among providers between counseling/psychotherapy and perpetrator treatment/education because the literature itself is at times confusing. For example, Scher and Stevens (1987) published an article advocating a psychotherapeutic approach in treating violence and in the same year edited a volume (Scher, Stevens, Good, and Eichenfield, 1987) with a chapter advocating an educational approach (Long, 1987). Neither publication draws a clear distinction between psychotherapeutic/counseling approaches and education. Long's insightful essay describes the nationally recognized St. Louis, Missouri, program Rape and Violence End Now (RAVEN), which is based on an educational intervention that illuminates violence for what it is. Treatment consists of education that challenges male socialization and control and examines violence within the context of that socialization and control (emphasizing, for example, that most rape perpetrators possess varying degrees of knowledge about the victim's state of mind, habits, and vulnerabilities, and that rape is usually not a random act). The goal of treatment is to stop interpersonal violence and to prevent the undermining of women's human rights.

Model Programs. A number of promising programs have been developed that use an educational curriculum. In addition to RAVEN, one of the first and very best is the Duluth model, which was developed for use in the Duluth, Minnesota, Batterers' Treatment Program and has since become a benchmark for treatment programs nationwide. The Duluth model differentiates between the role of the victim and the role of the community. It limits the victim's responsibility in initiating sanctions, transferring that responsibility to the community, and thus restricts the abuser's ability to manipulate the victim and the judicial system. The program's components, modified for campus use, include implementing policies that increase the use of university-initiated probable-cause judicial charges, bringing judicial charges with a signed complaint from the university rather than the victim; providing identified victims with safe housing and legal advocacy, and mandating assailant rehabilitation programs that focus on ending the use of coercive and violent behavior. This model illustrates how an effective treatment program encourages victims to use the judicial system rather than coercing them to seek counseling or placing them in the role of monitoring their assailants' behavior. Coordination of such resources as the judicial system, security measures, and administrative philosophy is necessary if an institution is to implement such a model successfully (Pence and Paymar, 1990). Further guidance is found in Barbara Hart's *Violent No More: Intervention Against Woman Abuse in Ohio* (1990), which outlines both philosophy and guidelines for implementation of a court-mandated program for domestic violence offenders that is responsive to the community. Hart's book presents an organized perspective on education-based treatment and includes guidelines for ensuring the accountability of treatment programs, and the perpetrators with whom they deal, to the women's community. Though not discussed in detail here, the suggested procedures for accountability are adaptable for campus implementation.

Treatment Within Campus Settings

Treatment must begin not with the dynamics of the perpetrator, but with the environment in which the violence occurred. Initially, any violent assailant must be physically removed from proximity to the victim. Precautions must be taken to ensure that she is not exposed to further danger. She should be asked how safe she feels within her living space, and safe housing resources should be made available. Temporary restraining orders and shelters are used routinely off campus to help ensure victims' safety; similar resources can be created and employed on campus. Sources of pressure on and control over the victim, such as financial reliance on the perpetrator, should be discussed to see if there are other ways to alleviate her concerns. It is important to ascertain the victim's wishes in these issues, as a victim will often experience imposed solutions as revictimization.

Treatment of the perpetrator should be mandatory and made available at no cost should he be unable to afford it. If the individual is brought up on charges in a court off campus, a university representative can be present to argue in favor of an adjudication that includes treatment, though not as an alternative to punishment. At no time during any perpetrator's legal process should treatment be considered an alternative to punishment. If the individual is found guilty through an on-campus procedure, university policy can insist that he complete treatment. Off-campus treatment is probably politically preferable to on-campus treatment because of the volatile atmosphere that surrounds campus violence, but should such off-campus treatment be unavailable, the university counseling center should step in to provide a safe and effective intervention. Successful completion of a perpetrator treatment program, whether on or off campus, should be necessary, but not sufficient, for continued attendance at the university. Suitability for continued enrollment

should be determined at the end of treatment and should include consideration of statements from victims and others affected by the violent act.

The goals of treatment for violence begin with getting perpetrators to take
full responsibility for their actions, not blaming their parents, circumstances,
or victims. They must also relate the extent of their history of rape, battering,
or other violence. The perpetrator must recognize the impact of his violence
on victims and others, as his ability to experience genuine empathy is central
to his understanding the impact of his behavior. He must also recognize the
impact that violence has on him and learn to forgive himself. The existence of
self-loathing should be explored because, though it may appear appropriate
given the circumstances, its presence creates one of the necessary prerequisites
for violence, the devaluing of self that is so often associated with a perpetrator's psyche.

Provider Issues. Providers who treat perpetrators need to reflect on their
own attitudes about violence and deal with questions of violence in their own
lives from victim, perpetrator, or witness perspectives, as appropriate. (Geffner,
Mantooth, Franks, and Rao, 1989). Personal questioning about the nature of
violence, what it is, and when it is appropriate, is critical for those who deal
with perpetrators. Attitudes toward women, men, sex roles, relationships,
anger, and conflict are all areas of personal exploration from which providers
will profit, especially when treating violent students.

Providers also need to adhere to certain behavioral standards to deliver
ethical treatment (Sonkin, Martin, and Walker, 1985). Providers should

- Be violence-free in their own lives.
- Be free of criminal convictions involving moral turpitude.
- Be free of alcohol or other drug abuse.
- Immediately report additional violence or threats of violence perpetrated by
  any client involved in mandated treatment to appropriate authorities, includ-
  ing university authorities.
- Report child abuse or suspected child abuse or neglect by a client as required
  by state law.
- Maintain open communication by discussing disagreements, problems, and
  issues directly with personnel in the divisions involved in violence intervention.
- Warn victims when the counselor believes a victim is at risk.

How the treatment provider views the perpetrator and the act of violence
is crucial to the success of treatment. Provider attitudes about rape and its relationship to sexual behavior and violence must be clarified. Provocation as a
rationalization for rape is often an issue for perpetrators, and the provider must
be clear that there are no behaviors for which rape is a justifiable consequence.
Rape is not a sexual act but an act of control and violence, and the treatment

specialist must be clear about this, or the perpetrator will remain confused about his actions. The question of justifiable violence is typical of the issues that providers must fully address. For some, the notion is an oxymoron while for others specific conditions, such as danger to oneself or loved ones, may justify violence. When is violence acceptable and Should a person ever slap a child are also typical questions that demand both the personal and professional attention of the conscientious provider.

The provider's goals and boundaries must not be blurred by the perpetrator. Benevolent confrontation and clear thinking are necessary, as the perpetrator's resistance to seeing himself accurately can be considerable. Any problem that a potential provider has dealing with perpetrators must be dealt with honestly. Feelings of fear, distaste, revulsion, or other impediments to acceptance of the perpetrator as a person must be clarified. The provider must work through and be clear about any personal experience as a victim, perpetrator, or witness, or he or she will run the risk of using the treatment for his or her own sake. Perpetrator treatment is not an opportunity to act out unresolved issues on the part of the provider, as this constitutes unethical behavior and professional abuse.

Treatment Modality. It is necessary for institutions to determine the form of treatment appropriate to the university and college setting: assignment to a primary individual provider, a group, or an outside referral. Making choices between referrals to individual or group treatment is complicated by the constraints of these two treatment settings. Individual treatment has the advantage of being flexible in terms of location. There is somewhat less need for structure, and such treatment can be less threatening for the provider. The disadvantages include the isolation of the provider, which heightens the likelihood that the provider's perspective will be co-opted by the perpetrator's perspective. Individual treatment also permits violence to be addressed as an individual issue, making it more difficult for the provider to address elements of social origin. Group interventions offer the advantages of dealing directly with the social issues of male isolation and supplying a healthy environment for confrontation and support and an arena for men to model appropriate use of power and control. The disadvantages of group modalities include the need to find an appropriate space, the need for multiple facilitators, and attrition due to participants' feeling their individual needs are not being addressed (Missbach, 1987).

Assessment

During intake of violence perpetrators, certain assessment steps are critical to ensure the safety of the campus as well as to maximize the chances for successful treatment. A lethality assessment should be performed. This is particularly important if battering is part of the perpetrator's history of violence. An alcohol and other drug assessment is always appropriate, and a complete assessment will also include elements designed to maximize treatment success.

Lethality. To ensure the safety of the victim, a systematic attempt to assess lethality in the perpetrator should precede all other interventions. First, the perpetrator's access to weapons must be determined. If access exists, this represents a clear and present danger to the victim, and providers should take action to remove the perpetrator's access to both weapons and the victim. The assessment should then consider the frequency and pattern of violent incidents in the perpetrator–victim relationship. Increases in either frequency or severity of violence are signals for concern. Similarly, the severity of a victim's injuries is a direct indication of the extent to which a perpetrator is willing to harm. Any threats to further harm or kill a victim must be taken seriously.

The lethality assessment should also consider the perpetrator's sense of ownership of the victim. Many men see a victim as a possession to do with as they see fit; hence, they are willing to rape, batter, and, in some cases, kill. Obsessive thoughts about the victim are often signals of potential lethality, especially if the perpetrator cannot imagine life without the victim. Though somewhat harder to discern, the centrality or level of dependence on the victim in the perpetrator's life is important to consider for the same reasons as the level of obsessive thinking. Fantasies of violence, especially of homicide or suicide, are significant and should be explored for their meaning and to ensure the absence of psychopathology. The perpetrator's level of depression is critical, as danger to self or the victim can increase dramatically as that depression begins to lift. Finally, sensitivity to those who have additional reasons for their identities to remain private (such as closeted lesbian, bisexual, or gay perpetrators who are desperately committed to secrecy) is essential. They may so profoundly fear society's intolerance that they would resort to heightened violence to prevent being outed (Sonkin, Martin, and Walker, 1985).

Alcohol and Other Drugs. Many men must begin treatment for alcohol and other drug abuse before they can begin to look at their violent behavior. This is especially true when substance abuse impairs judgment, inhibits decision making, or changes the personality. Violent personality change during substance use indicates the need for treatment for substance abuse or addiction. Although this chapter does not deal with assessment or treatment for alcohol and other drug abuse (see Kinney and Leaton, 1991, for this information), the importance of these services cannot be overemphasized.

Success in Treatment. The purpose of assessment beyond lethality and alcohol and other drug abuse is to measure the perpetrator's motivation for change and appropriateness for treatment. Providers should attempt to discern whether any secondary gain is inherent in any positive motivation to change, in order to discover to what extent a perpetrator's participation is merely goal-directed compliance, for example, to avoid additional consequences. Appropriateness for treatment can be further investigated by qualified providers through administering a mental status exam, the Minnesota Multiphasic Personality Inventory (MMPI), or other intake tools, such as the Domestic Violence Inventory (DVI) (Lindeman, 1991). During assessment, providers also explain the treatment process and make referrals to collaborating resources.

Assessment in domestic violence circumstances takes on additional dimensions but none that lie outside the capacity of counseling center personnel. The willingness to ask the necessary questions and to act upon the information obtained constitute the required skills to complete a useful assessment.

Treatment Curriculum

When a full assessment covering lethality, alcohol and other drug use, and treatment variables has been completed, the program curriculum can be implemented. The approach is educational and deals with methods of control that men exert over women. The purpose is to increase perpetrators' understanding of how the perpetrator process has been made to seem socially acceptable and how those in treatment have fallen into the pattern of perpetration. Forms of violence are discussed, including sexual, physical, and verbal violence. An important element in the curriculum is understanding the cycle of violence.

Cycle of Violence. Figure 5.1 depicts the cycle of violence experienced by couples in which abuse occurs. In stage I of the cycle, tension building, neither partner is willing to confront the other. During this time, outside observers often assume that all is well in the abusive relationship when, in fact, the abuser is storing up tension, resentment, and anger and is heading toward an explosion. Stage II is the abuse itself, a classic overreaction to current circumstances. Almost anything in the immediate environment can be experienced by the perpetrator as noxious, and all at once, he releases the tension that has been building during stage I and becomes violent, typically forcing sexual behavior upon or battering the victim. Stage III is the apology and feelings of guilt. It is during this stage that the perpetrator commonly seeks help, either voluntarily or through some form of coercion (court-mandated treatment for example). During this period, the perpetrator is often seen as genuinely sorry, and he acts as though he has reformed when in fact he is about to enter the tension-building phase once again. At this point, the perpetrator either learns to avoid violence and work on self-awareness or the cycle begins again (Gondolf, 1985). The cycle is an escalating pattern, in which both the severity and frequency of violence increase. A single cycle can develop fully over the course of an evening or over the course of years, but it always has the same effect: the perpetrator forces control and victimizes.

Gender Role, Gender-Role Strain, and Control. O'Neil (1990) defines gender-role conflict as "a psychological state in which gender roles have negative consequences or impact" (p. 203), and gender-role strain as "excessive mental or physical tension caused by gender role conflict" (p. 203). It is the vigorous internalization of the rigidly defined male role that is "the most salient

Figure 5.1. Cycle of Violence

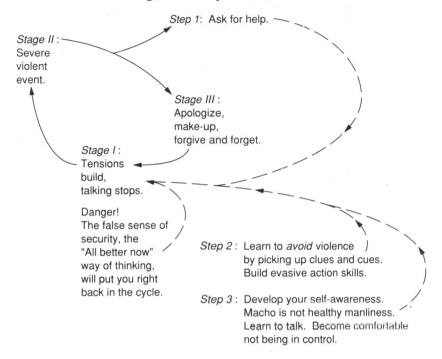

Step 1: Ask for help.

Stage II :
Severe
violent
event.

Stage III :
Apologize,
make-up,
forgive and forget.

Stage I :
Tensions
build,
talking stops.

Danger!
The false sense of
security, the
"All better now"
way of thinking,
will put you right
back in the cycle.

Step 2 : Learn to *avoid* violence
by picking up clues and cues.
Build evasive action skills.

Step 3 : Develop your self-awareness.
Macho is not healthy manliness.
Learn to talk. Become comfortable
not being in control.

Step 4 : Learn to *prevent* Stage I.
Learn to accept anger
through clear communication,
a community of friends, and
a new self-concept.

Source: Rape and Violence End Now, St. Louis, Missouri; reproduced in Gondolf, 1985, p. 54.

characteristic" of violent men (Hofeller, 1982, p. 14). It is precisely this characteristic that prompts Diana Russell to write, "Rape is not so much a deviant act as an over-conforming act" (quoted in Pleck, 1981, p. 146). (Male socialization and personality characteristics associated with rape proclivity are discussed in Chapter One.)

Treatment involves helping the perpetrator gain perspective on the cultural and societal causes of violence. Perpetrators learn that violence is a predictable response to the distorted belief that being male means being in control. When a perpetrator believes that another individual is responsible for his pain, he will attempt to control the individual rather than learn to manage his response. Attempted control, paired with an exaggerated male gender role, leads to violence. One likely consequence of traditional gender roles is that they teach men to view women as objects to possess. When this view is combined with the imperative to control all that is within his environment, including his partner, a man is at risk of becoming violent toward that partner.

Any loss of power or control within a relationship can be perceived as a threat by men who have accepted the demands of the traditional male gender role. The result is that these men will use any means to reestablish control, including violence (Marshall, in press).

Men who most feel the need to be in control are the most likely to experience themselves as out of control. Because our culture dictates that men be instrumental, atomistic, and fiercely independent, they are taught in treatment to counter those forces by reducing their isolation while increasing their feelings of awareness, power, and effectiveness. They accomplish this through assumption of responsibility for their personal behavior. Their coming to understand the dynamics of violence and gender roles is critical to this process. By becoming less self-controlling and more self-aware, the perpetrator learns to assume responsibility for his emotions and behavior, and thereby make the changes necessary to stop his violence.

In treatment, the interpersonal processes that support violence, such as isolating, intimidating, and threatening the victim, are identified and explored as controlling. For example, a perpetrator will often try to isolate a victim in order to maximize her dependency on him, control her access to support, and ensure that his behavior goes unwitnessed. He might intimidate through the use of male privilege, which allows men to move easily and without fear through society and, thus, permits a perpetrator to give the message that he is necessary to the victim's survival. Survival can be socially defined ("If you want to be popular with this fraternity, you gotta hang with me") as well as physically defined (offering protection in a dangerous neighborhood, for example). Threats and other forms of intimidation are techniques to elicit compliance from the victim. These processes are themselves emotionally abusive and are part of the escalating cycle of violence that can lead to rape, battering, and death.

Defense patterns that keep men from dealing with issues of control and gender-role strain include denying, minimizing, and blaming, all of which focus the perpetrator's energy and attention away from himself and toward the victim. As long as the perpetrator can falsely attribute his behavior to the victim, he can also blame her for her own victimization and never see, let alone deal with, his own process. Arguments with perpetrators that attempt to define the nature of violence as right or wrong often have less impact than pointing out that the results obtained from violence are too personally costly in both the short and long term, and that positive outcomes are available through means that are not controlling and abusive (Missbach, 1987).

Social Awareness and Skills. Often perpetrators are deficient in appropriate relationship skills simply because they were raised in environments that taught them wrong or abusive behaviors or did not teach them how to relate to others. They often have no understanding of compromise, sharing, empathy, considerateness, or many of the other skills that are essential to a successful relationship. Because communication, assertiveness, and stress reduction all play a critical role in successful coequal relationships, these skills, along with basic problem resolution techniques such as fair-fight, are taught to perpetrators in treatment.

Perpetrators must also learn to understand the connection between homophobia and violence. Fear of being labeled less of a man and a view that being gay is unmanly drive many men to commit violent acts to avoid the appearance or the label of being gay. Perpetrators must learn to make amends by working to achieve healthier individual functioning and productive interpersonal relations. Finally, they need to learn to assist victims in ways that are respectful, feasible, and welcomed and to support others in their efforts to become nonviolent.

Strategies.   Anger cues and physical signs that signal tension, stress, and the onset of anger are a perpetrator's first clues that he may have a violent outburst. Basic techniques familiar to most providers are very useful in creating perpetrator awareness of these cues. The perpetrator is asked to think about his last act of violence. What were the cues that preceded it? Had he practiced thinking about how he was going to corner his date and force her to have sex? Was he setting himself up for rejection so that he could create internal permission to be angry and retaliate by raping? Did he experience any emotions when he had these thoughts? Were there any important physical symptoms, such as sweating palms or pressure around his head, that preceded his feelings of anger? Once the precursors are identified, providers can help craft a plan of action that will aid the perpetrator to either talk himself down or to leave the situation through a time-out before the violence occurs. Teaching time-out procedures to those who are violent is essential if they are to learn to break the cycle of events that leads to violent outbursts. For those who have permission-giving thoughts, interventions designed to stop dysfunctional thought patterns are necessary. In addition, substitution of positive self-talk is essential to fill the void left by the removal of the negative thoughts.

Maintenance.   The final phase of treatment involves maintenance, during which a support system is developed for the perpetrator in order to prevent repeat violence. Friends, professionals, appropriately mature former perpetrators, and others in the community who are aware of the perpetrator's history should be available to him for support. It is through such support systems and through helping those who are learning how to manage their violent behavior that former perpetrators learn to give back to the community by preventing violence.

Program Research.   Because of the need for more efficient treatment of perpetrators and reduced numbers of future victims, research in the field of perpetrator treatment is critical. Programs implemented on campus should be followed carefully through research and supervised by those who feel strongly that treatment can be a powerful form of prevention. Successful off-campus rape and batterer treatment programs do not struggle with the difficulties imposed by class schedules, academic calendars, and student graduations, and yet even in these programs incomplete and failed treatment is too often a reality. However, new information is constantly being discovered that may further facilitate the treatment of violent clients. New findings have recently differentiated among men who rape, who batter, and who both batter and rape (Burkhart, in press). This information may further inform the treatment process. Meanwhile, research on the effectiveness of treatment programs must continue to discover what does and does not work.

Conclusion

The process of implementing effective on-campus treatment options for those who perpetrate violence will be difficult. There are those who are committed to avoiding the problem of violence perpetrators for many reasons, and their inertia represents a serious impediment. Affording perpetrators mandatory treatment should be part of any program seriously dedicated to ending violence. There are many ways to send the message about such nonviolent solutions to conflict as problem solving or mediation, and clinicians need to take the lead in devising new and effective means for reducing individual violence. The task can begin with an examination of training and professional practices. Practitioners' current lack of understanding about perpetrator issues and the exclusion of violent individuals from consideration as potential recipients of talented intervention are simply unacceptable, especially in light of the phenomenal cost to victims. University and college counseling center personnel have the opportunity to put in place an entirely novel approach to violence prevention, at least on college campuses. The result of inaction is easily predicted—more victims.

References

Bogel-Allbritten, R. B., and Allbritten, W. "The Hidden Victims: Courtship Violence Among College Students." Journal of College Student Personnel, 1986, 26, 201–204.

Burkhart, B. "Male Perpetrators of Sexual Violence." In L. Whitaker and J. W. Pollard (eds.), Campus Violence: Kinds, Causes and Cures. New York: Hayworth Press, in press. Also published in Journal of College Student Psychotherapy, in press.

Cerio, N. "Counseling Victims and Perpetrators of Campus Violence." Response, 1988, 11, 7–10.

Deschner, J. P. The Hitting Habit. New York: Free Press, 1984.

Deschner, J. P., and McNeil, J. S. "Results of Anger Control Training for Battering Couples." Journal of Family Violence, 1986, 1, 111–120.

Dutton, D. "The Outcome of Court Mandated Treatment for Wife Assault: A Quasi-experimental Evaluation." Violence and Victims, 1986, 1, 111–120.

Edleson, J. L., Miller, D. M., Stone, G. W., and Chapman, D. G. "Group Treatment for Men Who Batter." Social Work, 1985, 29, 237–242.

Finkelhor, D., Hotaling, G. T., and Yllo, K. "Breaking the Cycle of Abuse: Relationship Predictors." Child Development, 1988, 59, 1080–1088.

Gallagher, R. The Annual National Survey of Counseling Center Directors. Pittsburgh: University of Pittsburgh, 1991.

Geffner, R., Mantooth, C., Franks, D., and Rao, L. "Family Systems Approaches." In P. Caesar and L. Hamberger (eds.), Treating Men Who Batter: Theory, Practice and Programs. New York: Springer, 1989.

Gilbert, S. P. "Mandatory Counseling: An Oxymoron?" Paper presented at the meeting of the Association of University and College Counseling Center Directors, Minneapolis, Minn., 1992.

Gondolf, E. W. Men Who Batter: An Integrated Approach for Stopping Wife Abuse. Holmes Beach, Fla.: Learning Publications, 1985.

Hart, B. Violent No More: Intervention Against Woman Abuse in Ohio. Columbus, Ohio: Ohio Department of Human Services, 1990.

Hershberger, B. R. "An Assessment of the Effectiveness of Three Treatment Programs for Battering Men." Unpublished doctoral dissertation, Ohio State University, Columbus, 1988.

Hofeller, K. H. Social, Psychological, and Situational Factors in Wife Abuse. Palo Alto, Calif.: R & E Research Associates, 1982.

Jaffe, P. G., Wolfe, D. A., and Wilson, S. K. Children of Battered Women. Newbury Park, Calif.: Sage, 1990.

Kinney, J., and Leaton, G. Loosening the Grip. St. Louis: Mosby, 1991.

Lindeman, H. Domestic Violence Inventory. Phoenix, Ariz.: Risk and Needs Assessment, 1991.

Long, D. "Working with Men Who Batter." In M. Scher, M. Stevens, G. Good, and G. Eichenfield (eds.), Handbook of Counseling and Psychotherapy with Men. Newbury Park, Calif.: Sage, 1987.

Lore, R. K., and Schultz, L. A. "Control of Human Aggression." American Psychologist, 1993, 48, 16–25.

Marshall, D. "Characteristics of Men Who Abuse Their Partners: A Comparative Study." Unpublished doctoral dissertation, Ohio State University, Columbus, 1988.

Marshall, D. "Violence and the Male Gender Role." In L. Whitaker and J. W. Pollard, (eds.), Campus Violence: Kinds, Causes and Cures. New York: Hayworth Press, in press. Also published in Journal of College Student Psychotherapy, in press.

Missbach, J. S. Domestic Violence Program Guidelines. Skowhegan, Maine: J.S.M., 1987.

Neidig, P. H. "The Development and Evaluation of a Spouse Abuse Treatment Program in a Military Setting." Evaluation and Program Planning, 1986, 9, 275–280.

O'Neil, J. M. "Assessing Men's Gender Role Conflict." In D. Moore and F. Leafgren (eds.), Men in Conflict. Alexandria, Va.: American Association for Counseling and Development, 1990.

Pence, E., and Paymar, M. Power and Control: Tactics of Men Who Batter: An Educational Curriculum. Duluth, Minn.: Minnesota Program Development, 1990.

Pleck, J. H. The Myth of Masculinity. Cambridge, Mass.: Massachusetts Institute of Technology, 1981.

Pollard, J. W. "Treatment of Violence Perpetrators." In A. L. Renolds and M. von Destinon, (eds.), Campus Violence Handbook. Washington, D.C.: American College Personnel Association, 1991.

Pollard, J. W., and Whitaker, L. "Cures for Campus Violence, If We Want Them." In L. Whitaker and J. W. Pollard (eds.), Campus Violence: Kinds, Causes and Cures. New York: Hayworth Press, in press. Also published in Journal of College Student Psychotherapy, in press.

Roark, M. "Definitions of Violence." In A. L. Renolds and M. von Destinon (eds.), Campus Violence Handbook. Washington, D.C.: American College Personnel Association, 1991.

Saunders, D., and Hanusa, D. "Cognitive-Behavioral Treatment of Men Who Batter: The Shortterm Effects of Group Therapy." Journal of Family Violence, 1986, 1, 357–372.

Scher, M., and Stevens, M. "Men and Violence." Journal of Counseling and Development, 1987, 65, 351–355.

Scher, M., Stevens, M., Good, G., and Eichenfield, G. A. (eds.). Handbook of Counseling and Psychotherapy with Men. Newbury Park, Calif.: Sage, 1987.

Sonkin, D., Martin, D., and Walker, L. The Male Batterer: A Treatment Approach. New York: Springer, 1985.

Straus, M. A., and Gelles, R. J. "Societal Change and Change in Family Violence from 1975 to 1985 as Revealed by Two National Surveys." *Journal of Marriage and the Family*, 1986, *48*, 465–479.

Straus, M. A., Gelles, R. J., and Steinmetz, S. *Behind Closed Doors: Violence in the American Family*. New York: Anchor/Doubleday, 1980.

Walker, L. E. *The Battered Woman*. New York: HarperCollins, 1979.

Williams, G. H. "Perspective Transformation as an Adult Learning Theory to Explain and Facilitate Change in Male Spouse Abusers." Unpublished doctoral dissertation, Northern Illinois University, 1985.

JEFFREY W. POLLARD is director of counseling and health services and adjunct assistant professor of psychology at Denison University, Granville, Ohio.

Methodological problems of previous research on male perpetrators are reviewed and a new research agenda that examines men's prosocial behavior is proposed.

Research on Men and Rape: Methodological Problems and Future Directions

Barry R. Burkhart, Susan E. Bourg, Alan D. Berkowitz

Recently, several critics of acquaintance rape research have argued that much of the epidemiological data collected on acquaintance rape misrepresents the genuine level of sexual violence in this culture (Gilbert, 1991). These critics assert that "radical feminists have distorted the definition of rape and created a bogus epidemic" (Hendrix cited in Koss, 1992, p. 122). Koss (1992) has ably responded to these critics on methodological grounds, but these criticisms underscore the necessity for impeccable methodology, given the ideological implications of data on sexual violence. The value of rigorous methodology is always clear in social science research. When, however, research has implications for changing the values of an entire culture, the need for strong methodological standards is heightened. The meanings of data are only as clear as the methodology is powerful. In research on sexual violence, particularly research indicating a link between socially valued standards of masculinity and sexual violence (Lisak, 1991), the power of the finding must be beyond reproach. Otherwise, critics can deny the meaning of the data in their resistance to change. This chapter reviews some of the methodological problems of current research on males and sexual violence. In a previous essay (Burkhart and Stanton, 1988), we reviewed methodological problems of the early generation of acquaintance rape research. We are pleased to see that the second generation of research is much more methodologically sophisticated. Nonetheless, several basic areas of methodological concern remain.

The Achilles heel of research in acquaintance rape perpetrated by males is sampling. With the exception of the Ageton (1983) and Koss, Gidycz, and Wisniewski (1987) studies, almost all research on males and sexual violence has used convenience sampling procedures. Moreover, with the exception of Ageton (1983), almost all the research has examined college males. Though there are good reasons for using college males (they are accessible, at a high-risk developmental period, and usually compliant with research demands), it is clear that to gain the broader perspective necessary to generalize research findings more subpopulations must be represented. Economic and practical barriers to this research are considerable and, without the support of federal funding, are sufficient to prevent appreciable development of research with representative samples of males. Thus, not only must researchers be encouraged to develop this research but those responsible for grant-funding policies must also heed the call to support it. An additional sampling issue that limits the generalizability of perpetrator research is that almost all studies either sample white heterosexual males or do not ask the respondents' sexual orientations and ethnicities. Thus, more research is needed, first, to document the incidence of rape and sexual assault in populations of non-Caucasian and nonheterosexual men and, second, to examine the extent to which factors associated with rape proclivity are similar across these different populations.

Beyond these basic sampling problems, several additional critical methodological issues should be addressed. The most fundamental of these additional issues is measurement. In an excellent paper, Porter and Critelli (1992) have comprehensively analyzed the measurement issues involved in research on sexual aggression in college males, listing a number of specific problems with existing measurement procedures and identifying the following difficulties in particular: internal consistency coefficients of measures not provided; self-report measures not checked for veracity and replications of findings not provided; alternative methods (subject interviews or cohort interviews) rarely used; controls for social desirability not included in measurement procedures, despite data including underreporting of sexually aggressive conduct (Heilbum and Loftus, 1986; Koss and Gidycz, 1985) and evidence that social desirability moderates the self-report of sexually aggressive conduct (Porter, Critelli, and Tang, 1992); dimensions confounded in the assessment of sexually aggressive behavior, such as sexual outcomes (intercourse or no intercourse) confounded with the method of coercion used; data not obtained relative to frequencies of behavior or the number of victims; obviousness of questionnaires not addressed; and data not obtained relative to the temporal ranges within which aggressive behaviors occurred.

Echoing the conclusions of other reviewers, Porter and Critelli (1992) also argue the need for some standardization of measurement processes since the inability of reviewers to compare data from different studies owing to measurement variability impedes development of the field. Porter and Critelli also call for the development of instruments that will provide richer analysis of the contexts of sexually aggressive behavior. As suggested by Shotland (1992), elements of a behavior's context (a relationship, for example) may be critical to an accurate conceptual understanding of the behavior.

Porter and Critelli (1992) suggest that the current reliance on group correlational designs be supplemented by other forms or investigations. For example, Lisak (1991) illustrates how the sensitive extended clinical interview can provide rich qualitative data. This method already has shown considerable utility in research on incarcerated offenders (Groth and Birnbaum, 1979). We believe that the field has matured to the point where simple epidemiological research needs to be supplanted by more rigorous, theory-driven controlled research. As do Porter and Critelli (1992), we support programmatic research in which the variables implicated by correlational designs are tested in controlled studies. We understand that not all variables can be manipulated, so causal modeling strategies also will be necessary (Malamuth, Sockloskie, Koss, and Tanaka, 1991).

Finally, research on men and rape has focused almost exclusively on identifying the sociocultural determinants, psychological characteristics, and behaviors associated with rape proclivity. More recently, a second generation of scholarship has led to the development of sophisticated multivariate theoretical models that examine the causal determinants of sexually coercive behavior. While knowledge gained from this research has led to significant advances in the identification and treatment of perpetrators, much less is known about the incidence and correlates of prosocial, anti-rape behaviors among men. Such information could form guidelines for the development of effective rape prevention programs for men and encourage more men to confront and take action against peers whose speech and actions result in the objectification and exploitation of women. In what follows, we propose a research agenda to provide such a knowledge base, and we review preliminary research that can support and strengthen anti-rape attitudes among men.

Most studies of the frequency of sexual assault among college students indicate that from 25 percent to 60 percent of college men have engaged in some form of sexually coercive behavior (see Chapter One). Less is known about the 40 percent to 75 percent of men who are not guilty of perpetrating a sexual assault. What, for example, are the personality characteristics, attitudes, and beliefs of men who do not believe in rape myths, who strive for consent and mutuality in their sexual relationships, and who are uncomfortable with the rape culture that surrounds them?

Preliminary research suggests that many men may be uncomfortable with the sexist and objectifying language used by men in all-male groups to describe women. When asked to "describe something that bothers you which men do when there are no women present," over 75 percent of the 100 men participating in a four-campus survey indicated that were uncomfortable with the language men use to describe women or with men's talking about sexual experiences (Berkowitz, in press). Most of these men are ignorant of other men's discomfort with such actions, an ignorance that may prevent them from expressing their true feelings to other men. A second line of research has established that most men overestimate the degree to which their male peers are

sexually active (Berkowitz, in press). This combination of silence and ignorance allows a minority of men, those most likely to be perpetrators, to maintain the belief systems and myths that constitute the rape culture and prevents
the silent majority from speaking out against such actions. Clearly, more
research, both qualitative and quantitative, is needed to replicate these results,
document other sources of men's discomfort, and identify variables that can be
used to promote change among men. Berkowitz (1992) has suggested that men
may engage in unwanted sexual activity because of actual or perceived peer
pressure from other men. In one study, Muehlenhard and Cook (1988)
reported that almost two-thirds of the men surveyed had engaged in unwanted
intercourse, primarily because of male peer pressure or wanting to be popular. More research is needed on the types of peer pressure experienced by men,
the extent to which this pressure results in sexual assault, and the incidence
and types of unwanted sexual activity engaged in by men as a result of such
pressure.

Other lines of research might identify factors that increase men's empathy
towards victims. For example, Hamilton and Yee (1990) studied the effect of
different types of information on college men and women's rape-supportive
attitudes and rape proclivity. They found that while provision of information
about rape was not associated with reduced rape proclivity, greater knowledge
about rape trauma and greater perception of rape as aversive resulted in fewer
rape-supportive attitudes among both genders and a lower likelihood of raping among men.

In summary, a new generation of research on men is needed that will
enhance society's understanding of prosocial, anti-rape attitudes and allow the
design of more effective rape prevention programs. Such research could provide profiles of nonperpetrators; document men's misperceptions of other
men's actions and beliefs; provide typologies of male peer pressure, men's
unwanted sexual activity, and the correlates to these elements; and identify factors associated with increased empathy on the part of men for victims of sexual assault.

References

Ageton, S. S. *Sexual Assault Among Adolescents*. Lexington, Mass.: Heath, 1983.

Berkowitz, A. D. "College Men as Perpetrators of Acquaintance Rape and Sexual Assault: A
Review of Recent Research." *Journal of American College Health*, 1992, 40, 175–181.

Berkowitz, A. D. "The Role of Coaches in Rape Prevention Programs for Athletes." In A. Parrot,
N. Cummings, and T. Marchell (eds.), *Rape 101: Sexual Assault Prevention for College Athletes*.
Holmes Beach, Fla.: Learning Publications, in press.

Burkhart, B. R., and Stanton, A. "Sexual Aggression in Acquaintance Relationships." In G. W.
Russell (ed.), *Violence in Intimate Relationships*. New York: PMA Press, 1988.

Gilbert, N. "The Phantom Epidemic of Sexual Assault." *The Public Interest*, 1991, 103, 54–65.

Groth, A. N., and Birnbaum, H. J. *Men Who Rape*. New York: Plenum, 1979.

Hamilton, M., and Yee, J. "Rape Knowledge and Propensity to Rape." *Journal of Research in Personality*, 1990, 24, 111–122.

Heilbum, A. B., and Loftus, M. P. "The Role of Sadism and Peer Pressure in the Sexual Aggression of Male College Students." *Journal of Sex Research*, 1986, 22, 320–332.

Koss, M. P. "Defending Date Rape." *Journal of Interpersonal Violence*, 1992, 7 (1), 122–126.

Koss, M. P., and Gidycz, C. A. "Sexual Experiences Survey: Reliability and Validity." *Journal of Consulting and Clinical Psychology*, 1985, 53, 422–423.

Koss, M. P., Gidycz, C. A., and Wisniewski, N. "The Scope of Rape: Incidence and Prevalence of Sexual Aggression and Victimization in a Sample of Higher-Education Students." *Journal of Consulting and Clinical Psychology*, 1987, 55, 162–170.

Lisak, D. "Sexual Aggression, Masculinity, and Fathers." *Journal of Women in Culture and Society*, 1991, 16 (2), 238–262.

Malamuth, N. M., Sockloskie, R. J., Koss, M. P., and Tanaka, J. S. "Characteristics of Aggressors Against Women: Testing a Model Using a National Sample of College Students." *Journal of Consulting and Clinical Psychology*, 1991, 59 (5), 670–681.

Muehlenhard, C. L., and Cook, S. W. "Men's Reports of Unwanted Sexual Activity." *Journal of Sex Research*, 1988, 24, 58–82.

Porter, J. F., and Critelli, J. W. "Measurement of Sexual Aggression in College Men: A Methodological Analysis." *Archives of Sexual Behavior*, 1992, 21 (6), 525–541.

Porter, J. F., Critelli, J. W., and Tang, C.S.T. "Sexual and Aggressive Motives in Sexually Aggressive College Males." *Archives of Sexual Behavior*, 1992, 21 (5), 457–468.

Shotland, L. "A Theory of the Causes of Courtship Rape: II." *Journal of Social Issues*, 1992, 48 (1), 127–143.

BARRY R. BURKHART *is professor of psychology at Auburn University.*

SUSAN E. BOURG *is a graduate student in clinical psychology at Auburn University.*

ALAN D. BERKOWITZ *is counseling center director and assistant professor of psychology at Hobart and William Smith Colleges.*

An evaluation of videos and printed material that may be used in rape prevention programs with a focus on men's issues.

Resources for Developing Acquaintance Rape Prevention Programs for Men

James P. Earle, Charles T. Nies

Preparing an acquaintance rape intervention for men is a difficult task for a number of reasons. First, rape is a very difficult subject for men to talk about, and the idea that an acquaintance could be capable of perpetrating an act of sexual aggression is very hard for many men to admit. Second, program designers must consider that many of the participants may have been perpetrators in an assaultive episode. Third, men themselves can be victims of sexual assault. Some statistics put sexual aggression against men in the general population as high as 10 percent. These three factors make the design of a effective intervention program for men especially problematic. If an intervention is to be successful, the following factors must be considered. Strategies must be well thought out, including group size, audience (single sex or coed), program pedagogy (discussion versus lecture), and resources that will best enhance workshop effectiveness. Additionally, program designers and facilitators must be knowledgeable about group dynamics, facilitation skills, laws regarding sexual assault, human sexuality, counseling skills, and crisis intervention skills.

While some interventions are generally more effective than others, different populations require different forms of intervention. Groups differ in terms of developmental level, maturity, education, knowledge of the subject, and interest. Thus, all educators should consider in advance the unique needs of the group they intend to serve. Failure to do so could produce a workshop counterproductive to its goal. For example, some writers advocate that representation of both genders provides important interaction and sharing of information about both sexes (Parrot, 1991), but there is empirical evidence that this approach may incur negative results. Earle (1992), for example, found that first-year college men are not well suited to coed sessions and that single-sex groupings with all male facilitators are more effective in changing this population's attitudes about women and rape. (Literature that evaluates the relative effectiveness of single-sex versus coed rape prevention programs is reviewed in Chapter Three.) Therefore, it is clear that the first step in developing an intervention is designing a strategy well suited to the needs of the intended population.

Considerations of strategies for pedagogy, format, training, and implementation will dictate what types of resources are necessary or helpful. A variety of techniques and activities must be considered to evoke participant interest and maximize learning outcomes. Effective activities for facilitating discussion include videos, role-plays and other experiential exercises, rape scenarios, and lectures presented by authorities in the field, survivors, or perpetrators.

In this chapter, we examine two types of resources available for the purpose of training facilitators and conducting acquaintance rape prevention workshops: videos and printed materials (manuals and training guides). We also provide guidelines for using consultants and speakers. The resources are discussed in terms of their value in addressing different program objectives. Parrot (1991) lists five possible rape prevention program objectives that are also relevant to programmers working with all-male groups: understanding acquaintance rape, its frequency in the local community, and how it relates to force and coercion; exploring participants' feelings about acquaintance rape and listening to the other gender's perspective; exploring cultural forces that contribute to the frequency and acceptability of sexual aggression; understanding how both verbal and nonverbal communication contribute to acquaintance rape; and identifying prevention strategies. Additional objectives for all-male groups might include provoking men to take action against sexual aggression; understanding the relationship between power and rape; defining consent; and learning legal or institutional definitions and impli-cations. Individual prevention programs may address some or all of these objectives.

Videos

We have identified more than thirty videos that are on the market or available through agencies, colleges, and universities and that deal with acquaintance rape and sexual violence towards women. Such materials are proliferating as acquaintance rape receives more attention as a serious problem on campuses nationally. While we aimed to review the most significant pieces of work available, readers should note that there are additional resources that may be more suitable to the needs of particular programs. The cost of each video is not included because cost may vary significantly depending on the intended use. However, all the videos reviewed can be purchased or rented for less than $200.

ABC News 20/20 (producer). *They Never Call It Rape*. An MTI release, 1990. Distributed by Coronet-MTI Film & Video, 108 Wilmot Rd., Deerfield, IL 60015. (800) 777-2400.

This edition of the ABC television newsmagazine "20/20" highlights the problem of gang rape. Interviews with rape survivors, students, college administrators, and rape experts explore the shocking reality of women victims' revictimization in university judicial systems. The video also explores the problems inherent in fraternity culture that perpetuate this crime. The program was produced for a very large audience, perhaps most of whom have never experienced fraternity life. It would also be appropriate viewing for any fraternity. However, given the damaging image that it paints of Greeks, it is essential that a facilitated discussion be provided following the video to help the audience process the information presented. Also, since it characterizes fraternity life as evil, it may be quite threatening to Greeks. Designers should thus expect defensive behavior to be a natural response from this population. Encouraging the participants to examine how the stereotyped male culture in the video relates to their own could be a productive strategy for moving beyond the defensiveness. However, this strategy could be difficult to carry out in a large-group setting or a setting with both Greeks and non-Greeks.

Binghamton University (producer). *Aftereffects: The Pain of Date Rape*, 1988. Contact Lt. James Kavanaugh, Department of Public Safety, Binghamton University, P.O. Box 6000, Binghamton, NY 13902-6000. (607) 777-2393.

This video takes place on a university campus and is excellent for use with men. Its cast consists almost entirely of student actors, and it depicts college culture in a manner students can easily relate to. It also provides insight into the world of the victim and her friends. It does have an explicit rape scene that might be upsetting to participants. Facilitators should be aware of this and warn viewers of its explicit nature. A section that depicts a counselor from a rape crisis center visiting a residence hall meeting may seem patronizing and could be skipped over. While this valuable production is suitable for both sexes and intended as such, it is especially suited for male audiences for a number of reasons. It has the capacity to increase empathy for victims and is thorough in its portrayal of men's enabling behavior. The story line is general, includes a number of typical male–male scenarios, and is broad enough to allow for discussions on a number of issues, including the role of alcohol, male culture, how all men contribute to the problem of rape, the aftereffects of rape, and the definition of consent. This approximately thirty-minute film is the one used in the model rape prevention program described in Chapter Three and in the outline in the Appendix to this volume.

Dystar Television, Inc./Collin Sledor (producer). *Someone You Know: Acquaintance Rape*, 1986. Distributed by Coronet-MTI Film & Video, 108 Wilmot Rd., Deerfield, IL 60015. (800) 777-2400.

This documentary, produced and hosted by Collin Sledor, interviews convicted rapists and rape survivors, providing a view into a scary side of male culture. The interviews with rapists highlight the attitudes these men have about women and rape, while the interviews with rape survivors illustrate the devastating effect rape has on women. This thirty-minute video allows enough time for a decent introductory exploration of issues for both men and women and would be appropriate for mixed audiences. One concern is whether the interviews with convicted rapists would allow male viewers to distance themselves from the issue of male violence. This would happen if the men refused or were unable to relate the experiences of convicted rapists to themselves. If this problem can be resolved by the program design, it would be appropriate to use this video in single-sex male workshops, as it creates empathy for victims. Helping college men translate the male perspective portrayed in the video into their own worldview would be an important topic for discussion after they view the video.

Goshen Enterprises, Inc. (producer). Rape: It's Not Just a Woman's Problem, 1991. Distributed by Campus Crime Prevention Programs, P.O. Box 204, Goshen, Kentucky, 40026. (502) 228-1499.

This video, approximately twenty minutes in length, is a taping of an all-male acquaintance rape workshop. The workshop facilitator is Daniel P. Keller, Director of Public Safety at the University of Louisville. The video presents a number of statistics relating to violent crime against women before it moves into the workshop. The workshop pedagogy is a lecture, using charts and three segments in which victims and a perpetrator disclose their experiences. The lecture addresses several significant issues including communication, consent, gang/group rape, rape myths, and rape consequences. The video serves as one example of how a workshop for men might be conducted and, therefore, would be a valuable training piece for student facilitators or workshop designers. However, it is not an appropriate resource for an actual workshop with college men because the lecture format is patronizing, and having men in a prevention workshop view a video of other men in a prevention workshop is redundant.

John Winther Productions, Inc., for Lifetime Television (producer). Against Her Will: Rape on Campus, 1989. Distributed by Coronet-MTI Film & Video, 108 Wilmot Rd., Deerfield, IL 60015. (800) 777-2400.

This documentary is hosted by actor Kelly McGillis, a rape victim herself. Designed to raise student awareness of the problems facing contemporary campus life and to educate students about how to protect themselves as well as their friends, it highlights educational and security measures that colleges and universities can employ to prevent acquaintance rape. The video is more than a surface summary, as it explores the complexity of the problem with respect to rapists' attitudes and colleges' frequent reluctance to deal with the issue, and reviews prevention programs. A series of interviews with college men, rape victims, and security officers highlights the horror of the crime. This video would be a suitable training piece for paraprofessional counselors and acquaintance rape program facilitators. At forty-six minutes in length, it may be too long to hold students' attention in a workshop setting.

Not Only Strangers, 1980. Distributed by Coronet-MTI Film & Video, 108 Wilmot Rd., Deerfield, IL 60015. (800) 777-2400.

This video portrays a young woman's feelings after she is raped by a classmate, and familiarizes the viewer with the effects of posttraumatic stress syndrome. The victim experiences shock, disgust, guilt, and eventually anger as she moves through the process of filing criminal charges. The video is twenty-three minutes long and appropriate for mixed- or single-sex audiences. It is also among the older ones available, and its age is apparent in the actors' clothing. Due to the video's explicitness, if it is viewed in a mixed setting, we strongly recommend that the facilitators be professionals, trained to deal with workshop participants who may be rape survivors. If it is shown to a single-sex male audience, facilitators should be aware that the men may want to focus on the legal issues associated with the story. Legal questions and issues are very objective, and men generally prefer to concentrate on such issues, finding them more comfortable than issues related to feelings. Facilitators should thus make an effort to focus the discussion on the emotional side of rape if the video is to have any real and lasting effects.

Perry, Dan (producer). Sugar and Spice and All Is Not Nice, 1984. Distributed by Coronet-MTI Film & Video, 108 Wilmot Rd., Deerfield, IL 60015. (800) 777-2400.

This video explores how U.S. culture perpetuates violence against women, particularly through advertising and pornography. Rape survivors and counselors express their opinions of this culture and what needs to be done to break the cycle. While this video clearly speaks to acquaintance rape and other forms of sexual aggression aimed at women, it would serve as an appropriate resource for an intervention aimed at the broader issue of male culture. Because its cast includes people hurt by this violence, it is extremely straightforward and frank. Although valid, it is a condemnation of the current masculine culture and may be overwhelming to a conservative male group. It would be most appropriate for the more mature male college students, those who are comfortable enough with their own identity to meet the challenge the video presents. At nineteen minutes, it presents enough information to be thought-provoking but cannot be characterized as thorough.

Sexual Assault: A Chance to Think, 1984. Contact Lt. Cathy Atwell, Police Department, University of Maryland, College Park, MD 20742. (301) 405-5728.

This video is accompanied by a program guide that instructs facilitators how to use the video in a workshop format. All actors are students, and the video depicts four types of assaults: a stranger attacking a victim in a parking lot, a student exposing himself in the library stacks, a peeping Tom, and a rape at a fraternity party. After each scene is played, the tape is stopped to allow for discussion that focuses on the emotional reactions of workshop participants. The workshop format and video are intended for all college student audiences, but a major objective is to get women to think about how they should respond to these various situations. As such, these materials are not the most suitable for all-male workshops. In addition, the video is about ten years old, and the actors' clothing may distract college audiences somewhat from the more important issues being presented. These materials could be a helpful training tool to sensitize security officers to the issues involved in rape, in the likely event that the officers need to help a sexual assault victim.

Swarthmore College (producer). Acquaintance Sexual Assault Video, 1990. Contact the Office of the Dean, Swarthmore College, 500 College Ave., Swarthmore, PA 19081-1397. (215) 328-8365.

Produced entirely by Swarthmore College students, this video presents three enacted scenarios involving sexual aggression and four voice-only scenarios, three of which are read by women and one by a man coerced into having sex by a woman. The actors' conversation seems awkward at times, but the scenarios are realistic and cover a broad range of issues for discussion. Of the three enacted scenarios, one depicts an angry boyfriend who becomes jealous and then sexually assaultive, one takes place at a fraternity party, and the final one depicts a relationship that is about to change because one friend wants something more intimate. The value of this twenty-minute video is that it touches on so many different issues: alcohol, jealousy, fraternity parties, older men "hitting on" young women, relationships and friendships, and physical assault.

Printed Materials

In this section, we review manuals and brochures that are suitable readings for planning programs and training facilitators.

Adams, A., and Abarbanel, G. Sexual Assault on Campus: What Can Colleges Do? Santa Monica, Calif.: Rape Treatment Center, Santa Monica Hospital Medical Center, 1988. Contact Rape Treatment Center, Santa Monica Hospital Medical Center, 1225 Fifteenth St., Santa Monica, CA 90404. (213) 319-4000.

Aileen Adams and Gail Abarbanel's forty-one page manual is a powerful introduction to the subject of sexual aggression and rape. The introductory chapter has eight distressing rape scenarios that take place on college campuses. Most frightening is the lack of support that rape victims receive from college and universities. The remainder of the report describes what colleges and universities can do to reduce the incidence of rape and sexual assault, as well as ways for higher education institutions to respond appropriately to victims of violent sexual crime. This manual is recommended for all college personnel who work in judicial affairs, security, and residence halls, as well as other constituents whose work may touch survivors of rape. A new edition is planned for release in the near future.

Chi Phi Fraternity. *Chi Phi Fraternity: Pledge Educator's Guide to Sexual Awareness.* Geneva, N.Y.: Chi Phi National Fraternity, 1988. Contact Keith Stockman, Vice President, Chi Phi National Fraternity, 500 Pulteney Street, Geneva, NY 14456. (315) 781-0617.

Because most fraternities are under enormous pressure to educate members about sexual aggression against women, many have designed noteworthy programs to confront this problem. Some of these programs can serve as models for designers developing their own programs. Many fraternity programs rely on discussion prompted by reading rape scenarios or viewing videos. This particular program guide was adapted from Julie Ehrhart's monograph "Campus Gang Rape: Party Games?" The guide includes distressing rape scenarios, including a gang rape, which are intended to be followed by a facilitated discussion, statistics on rape, rape myths, and readings on fraternity culture. There is a strong statement from the fraternity about sexual violence. College officials should review fraternity materials for rape prevention programs, and should insist that facilitators be properly trained. Chi Phi also suggests that a college official knowledgeable about college policy be in attendance at rape prevention workshops to ensure that the right message is conveyed to fraternity members.

Cornell University's Male Sexuality Peer Education Program: Training Manual and Workshop Outline, 1988. Contact Cornell University Health Services, Gannett Health Center, 10 Central Ave., Ithaca, NY 14853. (607) 255-4782.

This manual is useful as a secondary source for designing training programs for acquaintance rape prevention program facilitators. The program has a number of general objectives and includes coverage of male relationships, intimacy, homophobia, and sexuality, and the workshop design, training exercises, and outline are noteworthy. Particularly valuable is a section on facilitator training that describes a ten-hour introductory weekend of activities and discussions designed to develop group rapport, promote personal values clarification, and create a commitment to the goals of the program. Because the success of a prevention program is largely dependent on the effectiveness of the facilitator, proper training must not be overlooked. This manual can provide some direction.

Johnson, S. *Man-to-Man: When Your Partner Says NO.* Orwell, Vt.: Safer Society Press, 1992. Contact Safer Society Press, New York State Council of Churches, Shoreham Depot Rd., Box 24-B, Orwell, VT 05760-9756. (802) 897-7542.

Scott Johnson's forty-one page booklet was written as a guide for men, with the goal of educating them about pressured sex, date rape, and sexual exploitation. It is very easy reading yet informative, particularly about male culture. This publication would be an appropriate handout for first-year college men at orientation, but staff should develop a session in which the students can process the information constructively.

Keller, D. P. Rape . . . Awareness, Education, Prevention and Response: A Practical Guide for College and University Administrators. Goshen, Ky.: Campus Crime Prevention Programs, 1992. Contact Campus Crime Prevention Programs, P.O. Box 204, Goshen, KY 40026. (502) 228-1499.

Daniel P. Keller's thorough and lengthy volume is an updated edition of his The Prevention of Rape and Sexual Assault on Campus. Exploring rape awareness, education, prevention, and response, it is intended as a resource for administrators who work on prevention and response strategies for rape. A chapter on education contains an outline for an all-male acquaintance rape prevention workshop as well as a separate outline for a women's program. Given its length and broad array of issues, the book is not an appropriate resource for students.

Ohio State University Rape Education and Prevention Program, Fight Back with Stop Rape Awareness, 1984. Contact Sue A. Blanshan, Rape Education and Prevention Program, Ohio State University, 408 Ohio Union, 1739 North High St., Columbus, OH 43210-1392. (614) 422-8473.

This manual outlines a workshop developed specifically for men. The program encourages men to explore their own beliefs, attitudes, and behaviors in the context of a rape culture and examines strategies to effect change. It begins with a general section that includes philosophy and purpose, the recruiting and selection of facilitators, and how to secure an audience. The last and most significant chapter (roughly thirty-two pages long), is a thorough outline of a men's workshop, including an introduction, definitions, exercises, and discussion issues. The workshop is two hours and ten minutes long, but segments can be omitted depending on the particular intentions of the college and the needs of the audience. Overall, this book was the most thorough guide for men's workshops examined in this review.

Parrot, A. Acquaintance Rape and Sexual Assault: A Prevention Manual (5th ed.). Holmes Beach, Fla.: Learning Publications, 1991. Contact Ginny Faulkner, Learning Publications, 5351 Gulf Drive, P. O. Box 1338, Holmes Beach, FL. 34221-1338. (813) 778-6651.

Andrea Parrot's manual is perhaps the most comprehensive one available. Its purpose is to assist administrators in developing acquaintance rape education programs, and the first two parts of the book are extremely valuable. Part one explores many of the general issues associated with acquaintance rape, including sex-role socialization, patterns associated with acquaintance rape, and recommendations for college policies and procedures. Part two relates to prevention and education, providing objectives and strategies aimed at certain outcomes. The final section is a thorough bibliography of books, monographs, articles, and papers. Portions of part one present some of the most important issues that men need to deal with, particularly in discussions relating to socialization, and these portions may be appropriate for student facilitators involved in rape prevention workshops while the remainder of the manual is geared more toward professionals.

Personnel Resources

Our purpose in this section is to briefly outline the rationale for using consultants and to identify when they can be useful. Consultants or lecturers should be viewed as one resource among many through which workshop designers can meet rape prevention program needs. There are clear advantages associated with inviting outside experts to a campus. The presence of these experts legitimizes and validates the program. Moreover, they supply additional knowledge and resources around an issue that has no easy answers, offer a perspective that comes from the substantive knowledge of an outsider who views a larger picture, and also capture a perspective untainted by on-campus political agendas.

Another advantage of using a consultant is the statement this action makes about a university's or college's commitment to address the issue of sexual assault on campus. Bringing an expert to campus for a day of training workshops, lectures, or strategic planning meetings can communicate the importance placed on the issue. Additionally, the action expands the credibility of the program, whether it is an existing program or just in the early stages of development. It is, however, important to invite legitimate consultants; those who are merely using the issue of rape prevention for personal exposure can do more harm than good. It also may be more beneficial to use a consultant who focuses on specific topics in the field, such as policy development, gender issues and power, specific populations (Greeks, athletes), or the rape culture and societal factors. Generalists can sometimes cause confusion and leave a group without focal point.

Finally, when considering whether to use a consultant, it is important for program designers to identify specific campus needs. With that information, in addition to using the consultant in a variety of settings while he or she is on site, a program designer can maximize the long-term effectiveness of the consultant's visit by hiring a consultant whose expertise matches the defined objectives of the college's program.

Conclusion

Although there are hundreds of resources available to colleges and universities to address the problem of sexual assault on campus, there is very little information available for programs aimed directly at men. Yet it makes sense that rape prevention efforts should concentrate on educating men because it is men who rape. This chapter has attempted to bring together in one place some of the resources available to college staff and faculty who share this philosophy. Additionally, universities and colleges need to develop appropriate policies, study the problem of sexual assault as it relates to their own communities, and develop sound prevention programs aimed at educating all students.

Acquaintance rape is one of the most difficult problems facing college administrators, and there is no one quick fix. Time and commitment enable programs to evolve into sound interventions that can make a difference. College staff and faculty must begin by defining objectives and identifying the resources best suited to facilitate those objectives. It is our hope that this chapter provides such direction.

References

Earle, J. P. "Acquaintance Rape Workshops: Their Effectiveness in Changing the Attitudes of First Year College Men." Unpublished dissertation, University of Connecticut, 1992.

Parrot, A. "Acquaintance Rape and Sexual Assault Prevention Manual." Holmes Beach, Fla.: Learning Publications, 1991.

JAMES P. EARLE is associate dean at Franklin Pierce College.

CHARLES T. NIES is residence life coordinator at Hobart College.

Appendix: Acquaintance Rape Prevention Workshop Outline for Facilitators

I. Do a warm-up. Briefly state the purpose of the workshop and introduce yourself. Then introduce a warm-up exercise, saying, for example, "Before we talk more about what we are going to be doing tonight, we'd like to start with a brief warm-up."
   A. Try this suggested warm-up. Have each participant state his name and then answer the question, "What is difficult about being a first-year male on this campus?" After the warm-up, briefly summarize comments and issues raised.
   B. Or use these alternate warm-ups.
      1. Have each participant imagine for a minute what it would be like for him as a man if there were no rapes anywhere in the world for the next week. Have each man introduce himself and share a reaction to the exercise.
      2. Have each participant introduce himself and answer the question, "To what extent do you think that acquaintance rape is a problem on this campus?"
      3. Have each participant introduce himself and answer the question, "What makes it uncomfortable or helpful for men to talk about acquaintance rape?"
II. Introduce the workshop.
   A. Say something about yourself and why you decided to become a facilitator.
   B. Review the purposes and format of the workshop.
      1. Describe workshop purposes: to educate all students about the problem of acquaintance rape on this and other campuses, to review appropriate college policies, and to discuss what we can

do as men to understand the causes of rape and prevent it from occurring.

2. Review the workshop's focus on discussion ("we're interested in what you have to say"), norms (no coming and going during the workshop, listen to what others have to say), length, and the following format.

   a. Definition of acquaintance rape; facts and figures.
   b. Viewing of videotape.
   c. Discussion of videotape and definition of consent.
   d. Viewing of videotape highlights (optional).
   e. Review of appropriate college policies.
   f. What men can do: wrap-up and conclusion.

III. Cover definitions and facts.

   A. Present these definitions.

      1. Sexual harassment: abuse, harassment, or mistreatment of a person based on his or her gender. Examples include cat calls, obscene phone calls, uncomplimentary graffiti, and so forth.
      2. Sexual assault: any form of sexual contact without consent (kissing, touching, and so forth), including rape.
      3. Rape: any form of penetration into any part of the body without consent, intercourse without consent (give legal definition in your state).
      4. Acquaintance rape: any instance of sexual assault (including rape) in which the victim and perpetrator were previously known to each other.

   B. Present these facts.

      1. In a representative national sample of over 6,000 college students from thirty-two institutions (Koss, Gidycz, and Wisniewski, 1987), 54 percent of the women reported being victims of coerced or unwanted sexual contact since age fourteen; 28 percent of the women reported experiencing an assault that met the legal definition of rape (forced penis–vagina penetration). Over 25 percent of the men admitted obtaining sexual contact through some form of sexual aggression or coercion.
      2. In another representative study, 57 percent of the college men surveyed admitted perpetrating a sexual assault (Muehlenhard and Linton, 1987).
      3. National statistics suggest that one-third to one-half of all women will experience a rape in their lifetime. (Note: the majority of these rapes will be acquaintance rapes).
      4. Use statistics from your campus if available.

   C. Facilitate a discussion. Ask for any reactions, comments, or clarification of statistics and definitions. Emphasize the difference between acquaintance rape as miscommunication versus acquaintance rape as an abuse of power and trust (that is, it is morally wrong to impose your wishes on another person). Miscommunication would not occur to begin with if some men were not interested in "getting what they wanted" independently of another person's wishes.

IV. Introduce and show the edited version of the video *Aftereffects*. Mention that the video depicts an acquaintance rape on a college campus and shows what the victim goes through afterwards and that, following the video, participants will have time to discuss it and hear comments.

V. Facilitate a discussion following the videotape. Draw out audience responses and discuss concerns, reactions, and so forth. Remember, your role is to facilitate discussion and draw out comments, not give the "right" answers. Try to use examples or call on participants so as to elicit a variety of reactions, impressions, and concerns.

A. Ask initial questions.
1. "Was the video realistic?"
2. "Were any of you bothered by the video?"
3. "What did you think of the characters and events portrayed?"
4. "What did you think of Don?"

B. Ask questions about discussion topics to consider.
1. "Did Don have a right to expect Anne to have sex with him?"
2. "What did Anne think would happen in Don's room and how did her expectations differ from Don's?"
3. "What types of pressure to 'score' might Don have been feeling?"
4. "What are some of the ways in which men place this kind of pressure of on each other?"
5. "What was the role of alcohol in what happened?"
6. "What did you think of the reactions of the other men [Bob and Lenny] and the role of male peer pressure [in the bathroom scene in particular]?"
7. "What was Anne's experience of this event like and did Don have any idea of how she would be affected?"
8. "Was consent present or absent?" "What specifically was Anne consenting to and what was she not consenting to?"
9. "What were the different attitudes and responses of friends?" "What is the role of male peer pressure and enabling?"
10. "How can we encourage men to take action to stop rape and confront each other?"
11. "How are other men affected when men like Don behave the way he did?"

VI. Provide the definition of consent. At some point in the workshop, the guidelines for consent should be reviewed and discussed. A consent model avoids technical and legalistic discussions regarding whether or not a rape occurred and helps men focus on what they can do to minimize their risk of perpetrating a sexual assault. Discuss how alcohol affects consent. Consent requires three conditions.

A. Both parties are fully conscious.

B. Both parties are equally free to act.

C. Both parties have positively and clearly communicated their intent.

VII. Do an optional rerun of key incidents in video with stop action. If you feel there is no time to review the video, or if you do not want to interrupt a good discussion, this section can be skipped. The rerun contains only selected scenes (do not rewind after first showing) including Don's raping Anne, the bathroom scene, Julie confronting Don, and the vending machine scene. Stop the videotape after each scene to emphasize points, raise new issues not covered previously, and discuss the scene.

VIII. Summarize relevant college policies.

IX. Conclude the workshop.

A. Summarize issues and points raised so far. Try to end with some constructive advice and summary comments.

B. Ask the audience to consider the following questions.

1. "Am I putting my own needs and expectations ahead of another's?"

2. "Am I assuming that my partner feels the same as I do without checking it out?"

3. "Why do I want intercourse? (Is it to satisfy my ego? Gain the respect of other men? Are there other ways for me to express my caring and interest in another person?)"

4. "How will I feel about this tomorrow if she says that she never really wanted to have sex?"

5. "How do I feel when other men brag about sexual exploits?"

6. "How can I respond when other men make jokes about women or make derogatory comments?"

7. "Can men be raped by other men?" (Mention that 10 to 15 percent of all men will experience a sexual assault or rape in their lifetimes).

C. Mention campus resources available in the event of a sexual assault or rape.

D. Hand out and collect evaluations. Explain that facilitators and staff would appreciate participants' comments, which will be helpful in planning future workshops.

E. Ask anyone who might be interested in being trained as a facilitator to speak with you after the workshop.

F. Thank participants for their contribution and attention.

References

Koss, M. P., Gidycz, C. A., and Wisniewski, N. "The Scope and Prevalence of Rape: Incidence and Prevalence of Sexual Aggression and Victimization in a National Sample of Higher-Education Students." Journal of Consulting and Clinical Psychology, 1987, 55, 162–170.

Muehlenhard, C. L., and Linton, M. A. "Date Rape and Sexual Aggression in Dating Situations: Incidence and Risk Factors." Journal of Counseling Psychology, 1987, 34, 186–196.

INDEX

ORDERING INFORMATION

NEW DIRECTIONS FOR STUDENT SERVICES is a series of paperback books that offers guidelines and programs for aiding students in their total development—emotional, social, and physical, as well as intellectual. Books in the series are published quarterly in spring, summer, fall, and winter and are available for purchase by subscription as well as by single copy.

SUBSCRIPTIONS for 1994 cost $47.00 for individuals (a savings of 25 percent over single-copy prices) and $62.00 for institutions, agencies, and libraries. Please do not send institutional checks for personal subscriptions. Standing orders are accepted.

SINGLE COPIES cost $15.95 when payment accompanies order. (California, New Jersey, New York, and Washington, D.C., residents please include appropriate sales tax.) Billed orders will be charged postage and handling.

DISCOUNTS FOR QUANTITY ORDERS are available. Please write to the address below for information.

ALL ORDERS must include either the name of an individual or an official purchase order number. Please submit your order as follows:
    Subscriptions: specify series and year subscription is to begin
    Single copies: include individual title code (such as SS15)

MAIL ALL ORDERS TO:
    Jossey-Bass Publishers
    350 Sansome Street
    San Francisco, CA 94104-1342

FOR SINGLE-COPY SALES OUTSIDE OF THE UNITED STATES, CONTACT:
    Maxwell Macmillan International Publishing Group
    866 Third Avenue
    New York, NY 10022-6221

FOR SUBSCRIPTION SALES OUTSIDE OF THE UNITED STATES, CONTACT:
    any international subscription agency or Jossey-Bass directly.

Statement of Ownership,
Management and
Circulation
(Required by 39 U.S.C. 3685)

1A. Title of Publication	1B. PUBLICATION NO.									2. Date of Filing
NEW DIRECTIONS FOR STUDENT SERVICES	(ISSN)									
	0	1	6	4	7	9	7	0		12/11/93

3. Frequency of Issue	3A. No. of Issues Published Annually	3B. Annual Subscription Price
Quarterly	Four (4)	$47.00(personal) $62.00(institution

4. Complete Mailing Address of Known Office of Publication (Street, City, County, State and ZIP+4 Code) (Not printers)

350 Sansome Street, San Francisco, CA 94104-1342   (San Francisco County)

5. Complete Mailing Address of the Headquarters of General Business Offices of the Publisher (Not printer)

(above address)

6. Full Names and Complete Mailing Address of Publisher, Editor, and Managing Editor (This item MUST NOT be blank)

Publisher (Name and Complete Mailing Address)

Jossey-Bass Inc., Publishers (above address)

Editor (Name and Complete Mailing Address)

Margaret J. Barr, Vice President for Student Affairs, Northwestern Univ.,
Rebecca Crown Center, Suite 2-221, 633 Clark Street, Evanston, IL 60208-1107

Managing Editor (Name and Complete Mailing Address)

Lynn D. Luckow, President, Jossey-Bass Inc., Publishers (address above)

7. Owner (If owned by a corporation, its name and address must be stated and also immediately thereunder the names and addresses of stockholders owning or holding 1 percent or more of total amount of stock. If not owned by a corporation, the names and addresses of the individual owners must be given. If owned by a partnership or other unincorporated firm, its name and address, as well as that of each individual must be given. If the publication is published by a nonprofit organization, its name and address must be stated.) (Item must be completed.)

Full Name	Complete Mailing Address
Macmillan, Inc.	55 Railroad Avenue
	Greenwich, CT 06830-6378

8. Known Bondholders, Mortgagees, and Other Security Holders Owning or Holding 1 Percent or More of Total Amount of Bonds, Mortgages or Other Securities (If there are none, so state)

Full Name	Complete Mailing Address
same as above	same as above

9. For Completion by Nonprofit Organizations Authorized To Mail at Special Rates (DMM Section 424.12 only)
The purpose, function, and nonprofit status of this organization and the exempt status for Federal income tax purposes (Check one)

(1) ☐ Has Not Changed During Preceding 12 Months	(2) ☐ Has Changed During Preceding 12 Months	(If changed, publisher must submit explanation of change with this statement.)

10. Extent and Nature of Circulation (See instructions on reverse side)	Average No. Copies Each Issue During Preceding 12 Months	Actual No. Copies of Single Issue Published Nearest to Filing Date
A. Total No. Copies (Net Press Run)	2,207	2,212
B. Paid and/or Requested Circulation 1. Sales through dealers and carriers, street vendors and counter sales	393	131
2. Mail Subscription (Paid and/or requested)	915	979
C. Total Paid and/or Requested Circulation (Sum of 10B1 and 10B2)	1,308	1,110
D. Free Distribution by Mail, Carrier or Other Means Samples, Complimentary, and Other Free Copies	91	91
E. Total Distribution (Sum of C and D)	1,399	1,201
F. Copies Not Distributed 1. Office use, left over, unaccounted, spoiled after printing	808	1,011
2. Return from News Agents	0	0
G. TOTAL (Sum of E, F1 and 2—should equal net press run shown in A)	2,207	2,212

11. I certify that the statements made by me above are correct and complete	Signature and Title of Editor, Publisher, Business Manager, or Owner	Larry Ishii Vice President

PS Form 3526, January 1991   (See instructions on reverse)